THE BEST BOOK OF

USELESS
INFORMATION
EVER

THE BEST BOOK OF
USELESS
INFORMATION
EVER

A Few Thousand Other Things You Probably
Don't Need to Know
(But Might as Well Find Out)

NOEL BOTHAM
AND THE USELESS INFORMATION SOCIETY

A PERIGEE BOOK

A PERIGEE BOOK
Published by the Penguin Group
Penguin Group (USA) Inc.
375 Hudson Street, New York, New York 10014, USA
Penguin Group (Canada), 90 Eglinton Avenue East, Suite 700, Toronto, Ontario M4P 2Y3, Canada
(a division of Pearson Penguin Canada Inc.)
Penguin Books Ltd., 80 Strand, London WC2R 0RL, England
Penguin Group Ireland, 25 St. Stephen's Green, Dublin 2, Ireland (a division of Penguin Books Ltd.)
Penguin Group (Australia), 250 Camberwell Road, Camberwell, Victoria 3124, Australia
(a division of Pearson Australia Group Pty. Ltd.)
Penguin Books India Pvt. Ltd., 11 Community Centre, Panchsheel Park, New Delhi—110 017, India
Penguin Group (NZ), 67 Apollo Drive, Rosedale, North Shore 0632, New Zealand
(a division of Pearson New Zealand Ltd.)
Penguin Books (South Africa) (Pty.) Ltd., 24 Sturdee Avenue, Rosebank, Johannesburg 2196,
South Africa

Penguin Books Ltd., Registered Offices: 80 Strand, London WC2R 0RL, England

While the author has made every effort to provide accurate telephone numbers and Internet addresses at the time of publication, neither the publisher nor the author assumes any responsibility for errors, or for changes that occur after publication. Further, the publisher does not have any control over and does not assume any responsibility for author or third-party websites or their content.

First edition : January 2008

Library of Congress Cataloging-in-Publication Data

Botham, Noel, 1940–
    The best book of useless information ever : a few thousand other things you probably don't need to know (but might as well find out) / Noel Botham and the Useless Information Society.— 1st ed.
        p.   cm.
    ISBN-13: 978-0-399-53428-7
    1. Curiosities and wonders.   2. Handbooks, vade mecums, etc.   I. Useless Information Society.
II. Title.
    AG243.B663   2008
    031.02—dc22
                                                                                2007034943

PRINTED IN THE UNITED STATES OF AMERICA

10   9   8   7   6   5   4   3

Most Perigee books are available at special quantity discounts for bulk purchases for sales promotions, premiums, fund-raising, or educational use. Special books, or book excerpts, can also be created to fit specific needs. For details, write: Special Markets, Penguin Group (USA) Inc., 375 Hudson Street, New York, New York 10014.

THE USELESS INFORMATION SOCIETY

Members of The Useless Information Society

Chairman
NOEL BOTHAM
General Secretary
KEITH WATERHOUSE
Beadle
KENNY CLAYTON
Chaplain
FATHER MICHAEL SEED
MICHAEL DILLON
BRIAN HITCHEN
ALASDAIR LONG
TIM WOODWARD
RICHARD LITTLEJOHN
STEVE WALSH
STRUAN RODGER
GAVIN HANS-HAMILTON
ASHLEY LUFF

SUGGS
MIKE MALLOY
MICHAEL BOOTH
JOHN PAYNE
BARRY PALIN
JOSEPH CONNOLLY
TONY COBB
JOHN MCENTEE
JOHN BLAKE
JOHN ROBERTS
BILL HAGGARTY
CHARLES LOWE
JOHN KING
KEN STOTT
RICHARD CORRIGAN
CONNER WALSH
JOHN TAYLOR

CONTENTS

WHERE IN THE WORLD

NATIONAL PRIDE

The Statue of Liberty's fingernails weigh about one hundred pounds apiece.

About 167 billion pieces of mail are delivered in the United States each year.

The Pony Express, one of the most famous chapters in U.S. history, only lasted a little over one year, from April 1860 to October 1861.

Approximately 1.5 billion miles of telephone wire are strung across the United States.

America's first stock exchange was the Philadelphia Stock Exchange, established in 1790.

STATES OF MIND

There are four states where the first letter of the capital city is the same letter as the first letter of the state: Dover, Delaware; Honolulu, Hawaii; Indianapolis, Indiana; and Oklahoma City, Oklahoma.

The state of Alaska has the most people per population that walk to work in the whole of the United States.

About 8.5 percent of all Alaskans are Eskimos.

Oklahoma is the state with the highest population of Native Americans. It has no Indian reservations.

JELL-O was declared the "Official State Snack" of Utah in January 2001, with the second full week of February declared "Annual JELL-O Week."

Wyoming Valley is difficult to find—because it is in Pennsylvania.

One U.S. state no longer exists. In 1784, there was a state called Franklin, named after Benjamin Franklin. But four years later, it was incorporated into Tennessee.

Hawaiian lore teaches that the earth mother, Papa, mated with the sky father, Wakea, to give birth to the Hawaiian Islands.

Minnesota has ninety-nine lakes named Mud Lake.

The state of Maryland has no natural lakes.

The coastline around Lake Sakawea in North Dakota is longer than the California coastline along the Pacific Ocean.

The state of California raises the most turkeys in the United States.

Oregon has the most ghost towns of any state.

CITY SCAPES

Reno, Nevada, is farther west than Los Angeles, California.

The worst American city to live in, from the viewpoint of air pollution, is St. Louis, Missouri.

Ropesville, Lariat, and Loop are all towns in Texas.

Brooklyn's name is derived from the Dutch name *Breuke-len*, meaning "broken land."

HOUSE PROUD

There is a house in Margate, New Jersey, that was built in the shape of an elephant. A home in Norman, Oklahoma, is shaped like a chicken. There is a house in Massachusetts that is made entirely from newspapers. The floors, walls, and even the furniture are made from newspaper.

Another house, this one in Canada, is made of 18,000 discarded glass bottles.

FOREIGN RELATIONS

One in every three people in Israel uses a cell phone.

One of the country of Liechtenstein's main exports is dental products.

According to Scandinavian folklore, trolls only come out at night because sunlight will turn them to stone.

Birkenhead Park in Northwest England was the inspiration for New York's Central Park as it was the world's first civic public park.

After Canada and Mexico, Russia is the nearest neighbor to the United States. Siberia's easternmost point is just fifty-six miles from Alaska. In fact, in the middle of the Bering Strait, Russia's Big Diomede Island and the U.S.'s Little Diomede Island are only two miles apart.

The parents of the groom pay for the weddings in Thailand.

Danish pastry is called "Viennese bread" in Denmark, and Spanish rice is unknown in Spain.

Although Argentina's name means "Land of Silver," there is actually very little silver there. It was misnamed by explorers who thought they saw veins of the metal there.

The desert country of Saudi Arabia must import sand from other countries. This is because their desert sand is not suitable for building construction.

In Tibet, some women have special metal instruments used for picking their noses.

Bagpipes, although commonly identified with Scotland, are actually a very ancient instrument, possibly introduced into the British Isles by the Romans.

Almost 30,000 tourists visited Antarctica in 2005, and that number is expected to increase to 80,000 by 2010. Antarctica has only one ATM.

Andorra, a tiny country on the border between France and Spain, has the longest average life expectancy in the world: 83.52 years.

In Tokyo, the cost of placing a three-line classified ad in the newspaper is $3,625 per day.

There are many kremlins in Russia besides the well-known Moscow Kremlin. *Kremlin*, meaning "fortress," refers to any major fortified central complex in Russian cities and can be applied to the government buildings in any Russian town.

Japan has 130 times more people per square mile than the state of Montana.

Mount Everest is thought to be growing vertically by about 1/6 inch a year: the two tectonic plates of Asia and India, which collided millions of years ago to form the Himalayas, continue to press against each other, causing the Himalayan peaks to grow slightly each year.

The per capita use of soap in Great Britain is 40 ounces per year. In France, it is 22.6 ounces per year.

Colchester Castle, built on the orders of William the Conqueror between 1069 and 1100, was constructed around the podium of the earlier Roman temple of Claudius, creating the largest Norman keep in Britain.

The most expensive commercial real estate in the world is in Tokyo. The second most expensive is along Fifty-seventh Street in New York City.

RELIGIOUS FOUNDATIONS

Construction of the Notre Dame Cathedral in Strasbourg started in 1015, but it was not until 1439 that the spire was completed.

There is a monastery in Ethiopia that can be entered only by climbing up a rope dropped over the edge of a cliff.

The largest Gothic cathedral is not in Rome or Paris, but on Amsterdam Avenue in New York City.

The smallest church in the world is in Kentucky. There is room inside for three people.

LONDON CALLING

With a population of 7.3 million, London is the largest city in Europe. The average household size is 2.3 people. London was the first city to reach a population of more than 1 million people, in 1811. It remained the largest city in the world until it was overtaken by Tokyo in 1957.

The tomb of Elizabethan poet Edmund Spenser in Westminster Abbey is said to contain unpublished works by his contemporaries who threw manuscripts into his grave to honor his genius, including works from William Shakespeare.

The exact center of London is marked by a plaque in the church of St. Martin's-in-the-Fields overlooking Trafalgar Square, but the actual point is on the corner of Strand and Charing Cross Road, near the statue of Charles I. There is another plaque on the wall confirming this.

The Monument, built to commemorate the Great Fire of London that devastated the original walled city in September 1666, was at the time of its construction the tallest isolated stone monument in the world. It is 202 feet high and is said to be 202 feet west of where the fire started in a baker's house, on Pudding Lane. Only six people died in the Great Fire of London, but another six committed suicide by jumping off the top of the Monument before a safety railing was added.

Brixton Market was the first electrified market in the United Kingdom and stands, as a result, on Electric Avenue.

The annual Notting Hill Carnival is the second largest carnival in the world after Rio de Janeiro's.

The tiered design of St. Bride's Church off Fleet Street is said to have inspired the traditional shape of wedding cakes.

Oxford Street is the busiest shopping street in Europe, having more than 300 shops and receiving in excess of over 200 million visitors a year, with a turnover of approximately $10 billion a year.

The original gravestone of the famous Elizabethan actor Richard Burbage in the graveyard of St. Leonard's, Shoreditch, is now missing but is often said to have read simply "Exit Burbage."

London's smallest house is only 3.5 feet wide and forms part of the Tyburn Convent on Hyde Park Place, where twenty nuns live. These nuns have taken a vow of silence and still pray for the souls of those who lost their lives on the "Tyburn Tree," London's main execution spot until 1783, where about fifty thousand people were executed.

The name Covent Garden is actually a spelling mistake. The area used to be the market garden for what is now Westminster Abbey monastery and convent.

The Houses of Parliament have nearly 1,200 rooms, 100 staircases, 11 courtyards, 8 bars, and 6 restaurants—none of them open to the public.

There is a nineteenth-century time capsule under the base of Cleopatra's Needle, the 68-foot, 3,450-year-old obelisk on the Embankment, containing a set of British currency, a railway guide, a Bible, and twelve portraits of "the prettiest English ladies." Incidentally, the obelisk does not actually have anything to do with Cleopatra, having been erected in the Egyptian city of Heliopolis in 1450 BC on the orders of the pharaoh Thutmose III.

Piccadilly is named after a kind of stiff collar made by a tailor who lived in the area in the seventeenth century.

The Tower of London's most celebrated residents are a colony of seven ravens. It is not known when they first settled there, but there is a legend that, should they ever desert the tower, the kingdom and monarchy will fall.

Only one British prime minister out of the fifty-one who have held the office since 1751 has ever been assassinated; Spencer Perceval was shot in the House of Commons in 1812.

In 1881, the Savoy Theatre became the first theater and public building to be lit entirely by electricity.

England's first printing press was set up on Fleet Street in 1475 by William Caxton.

The London Eye used 1,870 tons of steel in its construction and is heavier than 250 double-decker buses.

London is currently home to four World Heritage Sites: the Palace of Westminster, the Tower of London, Maritime Greenwich, and Kew Gardens.

Big Ben, known to most people as the four-faced clock tower of the Houses of Parliament, is actually the resonant bell on which the hours are struck. It was named after Sir Benjamin Hall, chief commissioner of works when the bell was hung in 1858. Cast in Whitechapel, it was the second giant bell made for the clock, after the first became cracked during a test ringing.

ROAD RAGE

The busiest stretch of highway in the country is New York's George Washington Bridge.

More than half of all Americans travel more than a million miles in their lifetimes.

American drivers average about 8,200 miles a year.

Twenty-four percent of Los Angeles is road and parking lots for cars. The city is the most car populated in the world, with one car per every 1.8 people.

In Kenya, people don't drive on the right or left side of the street in particular, just on whichever side is smoother.

Saunas outnumber cars in Finland.

There are more Rolls-Royces in Hong Kong than anywhere else in the world.

If you head directly south from Detroit, the first foreign country you will enter is Canada.

Japanese rickshaws are believed to have been invented by an American, Reverend Jonathan Scobie, who visited Okinawa in 1869.

QUIRKY QUOTABLES

FABULOUS FUNNYMEN

"I think in twenty years I'll be looked at like Bob Hope, doing those president jokes and golf shit. It scares me."

Eddie Murphy

"That's the kind of face you hang on your door in Africa."

Joan Rivers, on tanned fashion queen Donatella Versace

"You're about as useful as a one-legged man at an arse-kicking contest."

Rowan Atkinson

"I used to desire many, many things, but now I have just one desire, and that's to get rid of all my other desires."

John Cleese

"The one thing I remember about Christmas was that my father used to take me out in a boat about ten miles off-shore on Christmas Day, and I used to have to swim back. Extraordinary. It was a ritual. Mind you, that wasn't the hard part. The difficult bit was getting out of the sack."

John Cleese

BILL COSBY

"Women don't want to hear what you think. Women want to hear what they think—in a deeper voice."

"A word to the wise ain't necessary. It's the stupid ones who need the advice."

"I wasn't always black. . . . There was this freckle, and it got bigger and bigger."

"Always end the name of your child with a vowel, so that when you yell, the name will carry."

"I want to die before my wife, and the reason is this: if it is true that when you die, your soul goes up to Judgment, I don't want my wife up there ahead of me to tell them things."

"Did you ever see the customers in health-food stores? They are pale, skinny people who look half-dead. In a steak house, you see robust, ruddy people. They're dying, of course, but they look terrific."

"You know the only people who are always sure about the proper way to raise children? Those who've never had any."

"Old is always fifteen years from now."

"Human beings are the only creatures on earth that allow their children to come back home."

DAVID LETTERMAN

"There is no Off position on the genius switch."

"Traffic signals in New York are just rough guidelines."

"Charlton Heston admitted he had a drinking problem, and I said to myself, 'Thank God this guy doesn't own any guns!'"

"*USA Today* has come out with a new survey—apparently, three out of every four people make up 75 percent of the population."

"Wherever we've traveled in this great land of ours, we've found that people everywhere are about 90 percent water."

"People say New Yorkers can't get along. Not true. I saw two New Yorkers, complete strangers, sharing a cab. One guy took the tires and the radio; the other guy took the engine."

"I cannot sing, dance, or act; what else would I be but a talk-show host?"

"New York now leads the world's great cities in the number of people around whom you shouldn't make a sudden move."

"There is a new billboard outside Times Square. It keeps an up-to-the-minute count of gun-related crimes in New York. Some goofball is going to shoot someone just to see the numbers move."

ACTING SCHOOL

"Heartthrobs are a dime a dozen."
   Brad Pitt

"I'd like to design something like a city or a museum. I want to do something hands-on rather than just play golf, which is the sport of the religious right."
   Brad Pitt

"I'd like to put on buckskins and a ponytail and go underwater with a reed, hiding from the Indians. . . . To me, that's sexy!"
   Kevin Costner

"Any idiot can get laid when they're famous. That's easy. It's getting laid when you're not famous that takes some talent."
   Kevin Bacon

"There are two types of actors: those who say they want to be famous and those who are liars."

Kevin Bacon

"So you know what I'm gonna do? I'm gonna do something really outrageous, I'm gonna tell the truth."

John Travolta

"I had a huge crush on Olga Korbut, the gymnast. The only other person was Cliff Richard, which is embarrassing—it means that when I was seven I had bad taste and was presumably gay."

Hugh Grant

"With two movies opening this summer, I have no relaxing time at all. Whatever I have is spent in a drunken stupor."

Hugh Grant

"The moral of filmmaking in Britain is that you *will* be screwed by the weather."

Hugh Grant

"I am not the archetypal leading man. This is mainly for one reason: as you may have noticed, I have no hair."

Patrick Stewart

"I enjoy being a highly overpaid actor."

Roger Moore

"I tell you what really turns my toes up: love scenes with sixty-eight-year-old men and actresses young enough to be their granddaughter."

Mel Gibson

"After about twenty years of marriage, I'm finally starting to scratch the surface of that one [what women want]. And I think the answer lies somewhere between conversation and chocolate."

Mel Gibson

"I veer away from trying to understand why I act. I just know I need to do it."

Ralph Fiennes

"I'm going to marry a Jewish woman because I like the idea of getting up Sunday morning and going to the deli."

Michael J. Fox

"He's claiming abuse. I pay my wife good money for a little abuse, a good spanking sometimes. I don't know what he's complaining about."

Cuba Gooding Jr., on David Gest's lawsuit against Liza
Minnelli for physical abuse

"People have been so busy relating to how I look, it's a miracle I didn't become a self-conscious blob of protoplasm."

Robert Redford

"Health food may be good for the conscience but Oreos taste a hell of a lot better."

Robert Redford

"It was definitely different from kissing a girl. He had a bunch of stray hairs on his lip. The worst part was that we had to do thirty takes."

Jason Biggs, on locking lips with Seann William Scott in *American Wedding*

"The show was terrible because I didn't win!"

Frasier's David Hyde Pierce, on his 2003 Emmy Award loss

"We covered 'Hey, Jude.' My father panicked, misunderstanding the lyrics and thinking our lead singer was belting out 'Hey, Jew' to a roomful of Holocaust survivors."

Ben Stiller

ACTRESS ASSORTMENT

"I carried my Oscar to bed with me. My first and only three-way happened that night."

Halle Berry

"No one is more enslaved than a slave who doesn't think they're enslaved."

Kate Beckinsale

"If someone had told me years ago that sharing a sense of humor was so vital to partnerships, I could have avoided a lot of sex!"

Kate Beckinsale

"You don't realize how useful a therapist is until you see one yourself and discover you have more problems than you ever dreamed of."

Claire Danes

"I don't think I'm too thin at all. I understand when people say, 'Well, your face gets gaunt,' but, to get your bottom half to be the right size, your face might have to be a little gaunt. You choose your battles."

Courteney Cox Arquette

"Well, the joke is, of course, there is no British Empire left, is there? So I'm dame of a great big zero."

Dame Helen Mirren, on receiving a royal honor

"I have to be careful to get out before I become the grotesque caricature of a hatchet-faced woman with big knockers."

Jamie Lee Curtis

"From an early age I was aware of what America meant and how the Marines at Camp Pendleton were ready to defend us at a moment's notice. I also remember what fabulous bodies those troops had."

Heather Locklear

"I could serve coffee using my rear as a ledge."
    Jennifer Lopez

"Just standing around looking beautiful is so boring."
    Michelle Pfeiffer

"I know there are nights when I have power, when I could put on something and walk in somewhere, and if there is a man who doesn't look at me, it's because he's gay."
    Kathleen Turner

"I don't want to ever, ever do something in life that isn't fun. Ever."
    Jennifer Love Hewitt

"I've gone for each type: the rough guy; the nerdy, sweet, lovable guy; and the slick guy. I don't really have a type. Men in general are a good thing."
    Jennifer Aniston

"Angelina Jolie may get him [Antonio Banderas] in bed for eight hours on a movie set, but I get him in bed every day."
    Melanie Griffith

"In college I castrated twenty-one rats, and I got pretty good at it."
    Lisa Kudrow

"My favorite thing in the world is a box of fine European chocolates, which is, for sure, better than sex."
    Alicia Silverstone

"You can get Indian food at three in the morning, but I personally don't want Indian food at three in the morning. I want to go for a walk in my nightgown!"

Ashley Judd, on the pros and cons of living in New York

"Once you're famous, you realize for the rest of your life sex has to be in the bedroom."

Sandra Bullock, on her pre-celebrity sexual tryst in a taxi

"We're pleased he doesn't want to listen to the Wiggles—he just asks for the Clash."

Cate Blanchett, on her relief that her infant son, Dashiell, has good musical taste

"I'm not used to the *C* word. That is sort of a new deal. It is so funny. C'mon, I was not raised to take myself that seriously."

Brittany Murphy, on the novelty of being a celebrity

"I grew up with a lot of boys. I probably have a lot of testosterone for a woman."

Cameron Diaz

ELIZABETH TAYLOR

"Big girls need big diamonds."

"I don't think President [W.] Bush is doing anything at all about AIDS. In fact, I'm not sure he even knows how to spell AIDS."

"I fell off my pink cloud with a thud."

"I've only slept with men I've been married to. How many women can make that claim?"

"When the sun comes up, I have morals again."

"You find out who your real friends are when you're involved in a scandal."

GEORGE CLOONEY

"After doing *One Fine Day* and playing a pediatrician on *ER*, I'll never have kids. I'm going to have a vasectomy."

"I'm only two years older than Brad Pitt, but I look a lot older, which used to greatly frustrate me. It doesn't anymore. I don't have to fit into that category and get trounced by Tom Cruise and Brad."

"It [*Batman & Robin*] was a really bad film, I'm really bad in it, and it was the hardest thing to go out there and promote it by saying, 'There are things about this that are fascinating.'"

BRUCE WILLIS

"I'm staggered by the question of what it's like to be a multimillionaire. I always have to remind myself that I am."

"There are, I think, three countries left in the world where I can go and I'm not as well known as I am here. I'm a pretty big star, folks—I don't have to tell you. Superstar, I guess you could say."

"I've always had confidence. Before I was famous, that confidence got me into trouble. After I got famous, it just got me into more trouble."

MOUTHS WIDE OPEN

"What's the point of doing something good if nobody's watching?"

    Nicole Kidman, in *To Die For*

"People don't know the great things they [Scientologists] do, within education, and how they really try to help the community. It's just a very positive, wonderful thing."

    Tom Cruise, on Scientology

"Now I can wear heels."

    Nicole Kidman, on divorcing Tom Cruise

"The exciting part of acting, I don't know how else to explain it, are those moments when you surprise yourself."

    Tom Cruise

"There's no drugs, no Tom in a dress, no psychiatrists."

    Nicole Kidman

JACK NICHOLSON

"Once you've been really bad in a movie, there's a certain kind of fearlessness you develop."

"Just let the wardrobe do the acting."

"I don't want people to know what I'm actually like. It's not good for an actor."

"My mother never saw the irony in calling me a son of a bitch."

ARNOLD SCHWARZENEGGER

"I have a love interest in every one of my films—a gun."

"If it's hard to remember, it'll be difficult to forget."

"I knew I was a winner back in the late sixties. I knew I was destined for great things. People will say that kind of thinking is totally immodest. I agree. Modesty is not a word that applies to me in any way—I hope it never will."

"If it bleeds, we can kill it."

"I just use my muscles as a conversation piece, like someone walking a cheetah down Forty-second Street."

"My body is like breakfast, lunch, and dinner. I don't think about it, I just have it."

ELIZABETH HURLEY

"Hugh Grant and I both laugh and cringe at the same things, worship the same books, eat the same food, hate central heating, and sleep with the window open. I thought these things were vital, but being two peas in a pod ended up not being enough."

"Nothing irritates me more than chronic laziness in others. Mind you, it's only mental sloth I object to. Physical sloth can be heavenly."

"Being English, I always laugh at anything to do with the lavatory or bottoms."

"Up until they [children] go to school, they're relatively portable."

"I would seriously question whether anybody is really foolish enough to really say what they mean. Sometimes I think that civilization as we know it would kind of break down if we all were completely honest."

"I'd kill myself if I was as fat as Marilyn Monroe."

MODEL BEHAVIOR

"I never diet. I smoke. I drink now and then. I never work out. I work very hard, and I am worth every cent."
    Naomi Campbell

"I don't always wear underwear. When I'm in the heat, especially, I can't wear it. Like, if I'm wearing a flower dress, why do I have to wear underwear?"

Naomi Campbell

"They didn't even shoot my butt. Every now and again, you'll see a breast, but, like, big whoop! It's like, have you seen an Evian poster lately? Big deal, right?"

Daryl Hannah, on how painless her nude shoot for *Playboy* was

SINGER ZINGERS

"The biggest misconception people have about me is that I'm stupid."

Billy Idol

"All musicians are fun to get drunk with, except the ones who are cleaning up their act. We steer clear of those."

Rod Stewart, on intolerance for low tolerance

"I feel safe in white because, deep down inside, I'm an angel."

Sean "P. Diddy" Combs

"I'm taking my rats. Those are my friends for the tour. Thelma and Louise. They're so cute."

Pink

"Cameron Diaz was so cute at the MTV Movie Awards when she pulled her skirt up and wiped her armpits."

Pink

"It was no great tragedy being Judy Garland's daughter. I had tremendously interesting childhood years—except they had little to do with being a child."

Liza Minnelli

"In Hollywood now when people die they don't say, 'Did he leave a will' but 'Did he leave a diary?'"

Liza Minnelli

"I can't believe people got so upset at the sight of a single breast! America is so parochial, I may just have to move to Europe where people are more mature about things like that!"

Janet Jackson

"You have to be careful with the clitoris because, if the piercer doesn't know what he's doing, it can be numbed for good."

Janet Jackson

"Me and Janet really are two different people."

Michael Jackson

"I always had a repulsive need to be something more than human."

David Bowie

"It's tiny, what can I do?"

Ricky Martin, about his butt

"Craig David called me and said he'd written a song based on my song and asked if I'd like to come and sing on it. I asked my son, 'Is that cool? Is he cool?' and he was like, 'Yes, Dad!' so I said, 'Absolutely.'"

Sting

"I'm rich, freakin' rich. It's crazy."

Britney Spears

"I always listen to N*SYNC's 'Tearin' Up My Heart.' It reminds me to wear a bra."

Britney Spears

STAR-CROSSED LOVERS

"I used to do drugs, but don't tell anyone or it will ruin my image."   Courtney Love

"If it's illegal to rock and roll, throw my ass in jail!"

Kurt Cobain

"I found my inner bitch and ran with her."   Courtney Love

"If you ever need anything please don't hesitate to ask someone else first."   Kurt Cobain

"I'm not a woman, I'm a force of nature."   Courtney Love

"If you want to ask about my drug problem, go ask my big, fat, smart, ten-pound daughter, she'll answer any questions you have about it."   Courtney Love

MADONNA

"I think that everyone should get married at least once, so you can see what a silly, outdated institution it is."

"Children always understand. They have open minds. They have built-in [BS] detectors."

"Everyone probably thinks that I'm a raving nymphomaniac, that I have an insatiable sexual appetite, when the truth is I'd rather read a book."

"I'm tough, ambitious, and I know exactly what I want. If that makes me a bitch, OK."

"I won't be happy till I'm as famous as God."

"I miss New York. I still love how people talk to you on the street—just assault you and tell you what they think of your jacket."

"When I get down on my knees, it is not to pray."

"Sometimes you have to be a bitch to get things done."

"Everybody loves you when they are about to come."

"Better to live one year as a tiger than a hundred as a sheep."

"I have the same goal I've had ever since I was a girl. I want to rule the world."

"I am a survivor. I am like a cockroach; you just can't get rid of me."

"I am my own experiment. I am my own work of art."

"I always thought I should be treated like a star."

BARBRA STREISAND

"My biggest nightmare is I'm driving home and get sick and go to hospital. I say, 'Please help me.' And the people say, 'Hey, you look like . . .' And I'm dying while they're wondering whether I'm Barbra Streisand."

"I just don't like the idea of her [Diana Ross] singing my songs. Who the hell does she think she is? The world doesn't need another Streisand!"

"I hated singing. I wanted to be an actress. But I don't think I'd have made it any other way."

"Bitches. It's a very male-chauvinist word. I resent it deeply. A person who's a bitch would seem to be mean for no reason. I'm not a mean person. Maybe I'm rude without being aware of it—that's possible."

"Why does a woman work ten years to change a man's habits and then complain that he's not the man she married?"

KEITH RICHARDS

"I've never had a problem with drugs. I've had problems with the police."

"I never thought I was wasted, but I probably was."

"If you're going to kick authority in the teeth, you might as well use two feet."

"I only get ill when I give up drugs."

"Whatever side I take, I know well that I will be blamed."

DOLLY PARTON

"My weaknesses have always been food and men—in that order."

"I do have big tits. Always had 'em—pushed 'em up, whacked 'em around. Why not make fun of 'em? I've made a fortune with 'em."

"If you talk bad about country music, it's like saying bad things about my momma. Them's fightin' words."

"I have got little feet because nothing grows in the shade."

"Yeah, I flirt; I'm not blind and I'm not dead!"

"I was the first woman to burn my bra—it took the fire department four days to put it out."

"I hope people realize that there is a brain underneath the hair and a heart underneath the boobs."

"I look just like the girls next door . . . if you happen to live next door to an amusement park."

"I'm not offended by dumb-blond jokes because I know that I'm not dumb. I also know I'm not blond."

"It costs a lot of money to look this cheap."

"I didn't pay that much attention to the election. Nobody really grabbed me. The earthquakes in California worry me, so I'm hoping Arnold [Schwarzenegger] might take care of them."

OPRAH WINFREY

"Mr. Right's coming, but he's in Africa, and he's walking."

"Lots of people want to ride with you in the limo, but what you want is someone who will take the bus with you when the limo breaks down."

POSH AND BECKS

"I dress sexily—but not in an obvious way. Sexy in a virginal way."

Victoria Beckham

"Alex Ferguson is the best manager I've ever had at this level. Well, he's the only manager I've actually had at this level. But he's the best manager I've ever had."

David Beckham

"There are so many people out there taking the piss out of me that if I can't take the piss out of myself there's something going wrong."

Victoria Beckham

"If you haven't got it, fake it! Too short? Wear big high heels. But do practice walking!"

Victoria Beckham

"I definitely want [my son] Brooklyn to be christened, but I don't know into what religion yet."

David Beckham

"I want a big house with a moat and dragons and a fort to keep people out!"

Victoria Beckham

"My parents have been there for me, ever since I was about seven."

David Beckham

"I don't know much about football. I know what a goal is, which is surely the main thing about football."

Victoria Beckham

"I am not going to be no señorita."

Victoria Beckham, on moving to Spain

SPORTSMEN'S SAYINGS

"I can't really remember the names of the clubs that we went to."

Shaquille O'Neal, on whether he had visited the Parthenon during his visit to Greece

"Through years of experience I have found that air offers less resistance than dirt."

Jack Nicklaus

"I just want to conquer people and their souls."

Mike Tyson

"I owe a lot to my parents, especially my mother and father."

Greg Norman

"I feel old when I see mousse in my opponent's hair."

Andre Agassi

SPORTS SHORTS

PIGSKIN PARTICULARS

The New York Jets were once unable to find hotel rooms for a game in Indianapolis because they had all been booked up by people attending Gencon, a gaming convention.

The "huddle" in football was conceived because of a deaf football player who used sign language to communicate. The team didn't want the opposition to see the signals he used and in turn huddled around him.

Contrary to popular belief, the Cleveland Browns were likely *not* named after their legendary coach, Paul Brown. "Browns" was the second choice in a fan contest to name the team. ("Panthers" was the first choice, but unusable as there was a semi-pro team already called the Panthers.) Coach Brown stated that the team was named after boxing legend Joe "The Brown Bomber" Louis.

Hall of Fame running backs Gale Sayers and Barry Sanders were both born in Wichita, Kansas.

Atlanta Falcons quarterback Michael Vick and former Oakland Raiders quarterback Aaron Brooks are cousins.

The term "Hail Mary" for a last-second, desperation pass was coined by Cowboys great Roger Staubach, also a practicing Catholic.

Green Bay Packers quarterback Brett Favre's middle name is Lorenzo.

The Mannings are the only family to have had three players selected in the first round: father Archie by the New Orleans Saints in 1971, Peyton in 1998 by the Indianapolis Colts, and finally Eli in 2004 by the New York Giants.

Many have heard of or seen "the play," in which the Cal Bears threw five laterals to pull off a last-second upset of archrival Stanford. Few, however, know that Stanford's quarterback in that game was none other than Broncos legend John Elway.

Though Walter Payton and Gale Sayers are certainly two of the greatest backs of all time, it is the lesser-known Ernie Nevers who holds the Bears record for most rushing touchdowns in a single game, with six.

George O'Leary was head coach at Notre Dame for only five days before being forced to resign due to a falsehood on his résumé.

SHOTS FROM THE ROUGH

The only golf course on the island of Tonga has fifteen holes, and there's no penalty if a monkey steals your golf ball.

The first golf rule booklet was published in Scotland in 1754.

Golf great Billy Casper perfected his game during the Korean War while serving in the navy. Casper was assigned to operate and build golf driving ranges in the San Diego area.

Not all golf balls have 360 dimples. Most have anywhere from 300 to 450 dimples. The record holder was a ball with 1,070 dimples. The only odd-numbered dimpled ball on sale today has 333 dimples—all other balls have an even number of dimples. There are also many different kinds of dimple patterns.

The fastest golf drive is 120 miles per hour and was set by Gene Sarazen.

Tiger Woods is the only professional golfer to hold all four major championships at one time, although it did not happen in a single calendar year. He also currently holds the scoring record for all four majors.

Ernie Els's real name is Theodore.

There are more recreational golfers per capita in Canada than in any other country in the world.

When the golf ball was introduced in 1848, it was called a "gutta-percha" ball because its core was made from that tropical tree's sap.

The chances of making two holes-in-one in a round of golf are 1 in 67 million.

SLIPPED DISCS

In the 1870s, William Russell Frisbie opened a bakery called the Frisbie Pie Company in Bridgeport, Connecticut. His lightweight pie tins were embossed with the family name. College students started tossing and catching the empty tins as a pastime.

In the United States, more Frisbee discs are sold each year than baseballs, basketballs, and footballs combined.

PENALTY KICKS

Before soccer referees started using whistles in 1878, they used to rely on waving a handkerchief.

Belgian soccer team FC Wijtschale once gave up fifty-eight goals in just two games.

A female photographer has been banned from flying with the Romanian national soccer team because of superstitions that women could bring bad luck.

A man from Medellin, Colombia, has legally changed his name to Deportivo Independiente Medellin, after his favorite soccer team.

British soccer squad Chelsea Football Club received a set of tanning beds as training aids.

British team Norwich City was once urged to wear red underpants to help them win a game when they were in last place.

Brazilian soccer star Ronaldinho smashed a window at a twelfth-century cathedral by bungling an overhead kick while filming a commercial.

BECKHAM BITS

The study of David Beckham is part of a twelve-week "football culture" module for a university-degree course at Staffordshire University.

David Beckham is not a beer drinker, but prefers a nice glass of wine or Pepsi.

David Beckham has wife Victoria's name—albeit misspelled—in Hindi tattooed on his arm. She has "DB" tattooed on her wrist.

An experiment at Manchester United showed that David Beckham ran an average 8.8 miles per game—more than any other player on the team.

A careful medical examination revealed that David Beckham has one leg shorter than the other. However, a shoe insert to eradicate the problem proved too uncomfortable, so he stopped using it.

David Beckham's father missed his son's home debut for Real Madrid after losing his passport.

David Beckham wears a new pair of soccer cleats for every game he plays at an estimated cost of $600 a pair.

FAT CHANCE

To bulk up, sumo wrestlers eat huge portions of protein-rich stews called *chankonabe*, packed with fish or meat and vegetables, plus vast quantities of less healthy foods, including fast food. They often force themselves to eat when they are full, and they have a nap after lunch, thus acquiring flab on top of their strong muscles, which helps to keep their center of gravity low.

In 1988, the heaviest sumo wrestler ever recorded weighed in at a thundering 560 pounds.

LOOSE BALLS

There is a regulation-size half-court where employees can play basketball inside the Matterhorn at Disneyland.

In the 1987–88 NBA season, the shortest and tallest players in NBA history played together on the Washington Bullets. Tyrone "Muggsy" Bogues stood only 5'3", while his teammate Manute Bol towered over the competition at 7'7".

The iconic NBA logo design of a player's silhouette was based on Los Angeles Lakers great Jerry West.

The NCAA banned dunking in college basketball from 1967 to 1976, largely as a reaction to the dominance of UCLA center Lew Alcindor—who later changed his name to Kareem Abdul-Jabbar.

In China, a rough translation led to the Chicago Bulls being known as the "Red Oxen."

In 1988, the expansion Charlotte Hornets became the first team in major-league sports to be named after an insect.

In 1996–97, Robert Parish became the oldest active player in NBA history. He played for the Chicago Bulls at the ripe old age of forty-three.

HOOPSTER ALTER EGOS

Larry Johnson: "Grandmama"

Charles Barkley: "The Round Mound of Rebound"

Damon Stoudamire: "Mighty Mouse"

Vinnie Johnson: "The Microwave"

George Gervin: "The Iceman"

Darrell Griffith: "Dr. Dunkenstein"

John Wooden: "The Wizard of Westwood"

PECULIAR PURSUITS

A traditional sport on Nauru, a small Pacific island, is lassoing flying birds.

Vaimonkanto, or "wife carrying," is a popular sport. The championship games are held annually in Sonka-jarvi, Finland.

Enthusiasts of a "sport" called extreme ironing are trying to get Olympic recognition by showing off their ironing skills in extreme places like Times Square, Mount Rushmore, and even underwater.

"Hot cockles" was a popular game at Christmas in medieval times. Players took turns striking a blindfolded player, who had to guess the name of the person delivering each blow.

WILD PITCHES

One of Hall of Fame pitcher Nolan Ryan's jockstraps sold at auction for $25,000.

Hefty slugger Cecil Fielder went more than one thousand games without a stolen base until 1995, when he swiped his first bag after an errant throw from the catcher and a juggled catch by the second baseman.

Two father-son combinations have played in the same lineup: Ken Griffey Sr. and Ken Griffey Jr., and Tim Raines Sr. and Tim Raines Jr. However, the Griffeys are the only father-son combination to hit back-to-back homers, which they did in 1990.

Former Baltimore Orioles manager Earl Weaver holds the record for ejections with ninety-seven.

In 1941, Ted Williams became the last player to hit .400 for a season (he hit .406), but lost out in the American League MVP race to Yankee rival Joe DiMaggio.

Johnny Plessey batted .331 for the Cleveland Spiders in 1891, even though he spent the entire season batting with a rolled-up, lacquered copy of the *Toledo Post-Dispatch*.

YANKEE CLIPS

In July 1934, Babe Ruth paid a fan $20 for the return of the baseball he hit for his 700th career home run.

In 1964, for the tenth time in his major-league baseball career, Mickey Mantle hit home runs from both the left and right sides of the plate in the same game—setting a new baseball record.

Owner George Steinbrenner and Manager Billy Martin had a turbulent relationship. From 1975 to 1988, Steinbrenner hired and subsequently fired Martin *four* separate times.

Future NFL great John Elway spent two years in the Yankees' farm system before embarking on his celebrated career with the Denver Broncos.

WORLDLY WISE . . .

In the 1988 Calgary Olympics, ski jumper Eddie "The Eagle" Edwards finished fifty-eighth (last) in the 70-meter jump and fifty-fifth (last) in the 90-meter jump.

A helicopter installed the world's largest Olympic torch on top of the Calgary tower. The flame was visible for 10 to 12 miles and required 30,000 cubic feet of natural gas per hour.

In 1969, a brief skirmish broke out between Honduras and El Salvador. Although tensions had been heightened between the two countries, the conflict is often referred to as "The Football War" due to rioting during the qualifying matches of the 1970 FIFA World Cup. The actual war lasted only four days before a cease-fire was declared.

Around 18 million more text messages than normal were sent on the day England clinched victory against Australia in the 2003 Rugby World Cup final.

HIS AND HERS

When a male skier falls down, he tends to fall on his face. A woman skier tends to fall on her back.

Men are more streamlined than women for swimming, because the female's breasts create a lot of drag. Enough, in fact, that racing suits have been developed with tiny pegs above the breasts to cause disturbance, which decreases the drag.

PARLOR GAMES

If you add up the letters in all the names of the cards in one suit of the deck (ace, two, etc.), the total number of letters is fifty-two, the same as the number of cards in the deck.

In 2003 former world chess champion Ruslan Ponomariov became the first player to be disqualified at a major event after his cell phone rang during a game.

The longest Monopoly game in a bathtub was ninety-nine hours long. The longest game ever played was 1,680 hours (seventy days).

Table tennis was originally played in England in the 1880s with balls made from champagne corks and paddles made from cigar-box lids.

NET GAINS

The sport of volleyball was originally known as mintonette.

Tennis pro Evonne Goolagong's last name means "kangaroo's nose" in Australia's aboriginal language.

Michael Sangster, who played in the 1960s, had tennis's fastest serve, once clocked at 154 miles per hour.

Tennis great Goran Ivanisevic's father once crashed his $4 million yacht, not long after a friend totaled his $200,000 Porsche.

The longest singles match in tennis history took place in 1982 at the Davis Cup quarterfinals. John McEnroe and Mats Wilander battled for six hours and thirty-two minutes, with McEnroe finally emerging as the victor.

RACY DETAILS

A NASCAR fan once sent more than half a million emails to Fox because they'd shown a baseball game instead of a scheduled race.

Go-karting originated in 1956 when Art Ingels built the first kart in Southern California.

At 101, Larry Lewis ran the 100-yard dash in 17.8 seconds, setting a new world record for runners one hundred years old or older.

Horseracing is one of the most dangerous sports. Between two and three jockeys are killed each year. That's about how many baseball players have died in baseball's entire professional history.

EGGHEAD ESOTERICA

INVENTION MENTIONS

The screwdriver was invented before the screw.

Two common objects have the same function, but one has thousands of moving parts, while the other has absolutely no moving parts—an hourglass and a sundial.

The earliest known image of a fishing reel is from Chinese records circa AD 1195.

Silly Putty was invented in 1943 by an engineer at General Electric named James Wright, who was looking to create a substitute for natural rubber, which was difficult to obtain during World War II. The compound was created by combining silicone oil with boric acid. It did not end up being viable as a rubber substitute, but caught on as a novelty when a toy seller introduced it at the 1950 International Toy Fair.

The largest concrete structure in the United States is the Grand Coulee Dam on the Columbia River in Washington. Three times the bulk of the Hoover Dam and four times the volume of the Great Pyramid, it is nearly a mile long and 550 feet high—more than twice as tall as Niagara Falls. Its thirty-acre base is 500 feet wide and it consumed 12 million cubic yards of concrete.

In 1924, Clarence Birdseye invented the quick-freezing method, which allows us to enjoy delicious frozen dinners to this day.

MOTHERS OF INVENTION

The first disposable diaper was patented in 1946 by housewife Marion Donovan.

Kevlar, the material used in bulletproof vests, was invented in 1965 by Stephanie Kwolek, a researcher for the DuPont Company.

In 1905, prior even to the production of Ford's Model A, Mary Anderson received a patent for manual windshield wipers.

The test used to assess a newborn's health is known as an Apgar Score, so called in honor of its inventor, Dr. Virginia Apgar.

THE LATEST DEVELOPMENTS

James Dyson has invented a vacuum cleaner that can order its own spare parts.

A German supermarket chain has introduced a new way of allowing customers to pay using just their fingerprints.

Insurance company Esure announced plans to use voice-stress-analysis technology to weed out fraudulent claims.

Scientists in Australia have found that rotten bananas could provide enough energy for five hundred homes.

A German-based doctor has invented breast implants made from titanium.

Scientists in Australia have developed software that allows people to log on to personal computers by laughing.

The newest trend in the Netherlands is having tiny jewels implanted directly into the eye.

The first plan in the United Kingdom that allows drivers to pay for parking by cell phone was launched in Scotland.

Russian scientists have developed a new drug that prolongs drunkenness and enhances intoxication.

A German company has built the world's first washing machine that talks and recognizes spoken commands.

SURGICAL SILLINESS

Scientists have performed a surgical operation on a single living cell, using a needle that is just a few millionths of a meter wide.

Researchers have found that doctors who spend at least three hours a week playing video games make about 37 percent fewer mistakes in laparoscopic surgery than surgeons who didn't play video games at all.

CELL IT

As much as 80 percent of microwaves from cell phones are said to be absorbed by your head.

A Belgian couple got married by short message service (SMS) because text messaging played such a big part in their relationship.

Approximately 1,314 phone calls are misplaced by telecom services every minute.

There are 150 million cell phones in use in the United States, more than one for every two human beings in the country.

More than 50 percent of the people in the world have never made or received a telephone call.

I'M A MAC. AND I'M A PC . . .

The "save" icon on Microsoft Word shows a floppy disk with the shutter on backward.

Every five seconds a computer is infected with a virus.

The first microcomputer was called the Altair 8800 and was made by a company called MITS in 1974. It came in a kit and had to be assembled by the user.

IBM introduced their first personal computer in 1981.

The basis of the Macintosh computer was Apple's Lisa, which was released in 1983. This was the first system to utilize a GUI, or graphical user interface. The first Macintosh was released in 1984.

The name Intel stems from the company's former name, Integrated Electronics.

IT'S LIKE A SERIES OF TUBES . . .

The annual growth of Internet traffic is 314,000 percent.

Thirty-two percent of singles think they will meet their future mate online.

A remote tribe in the Brazilian jungle is now online after a charity gave them five battery-powered computers.

The Church of England has appointed its first web pastor to oversee a new parish that will exist only on the net.

Thirty-five billion emails are sent each day throughout the world.

The first domain name ever registered was Symbolics .com.

Every single "all-a" domain name, from a.com to aaaaaaaaaaaaaaaaaaaaaaaaaaaaaaaaaaaaaaaaaaaaaaaaaaaaaaaa aaaaaaaaaa.com (63 a's), has been registered.

Every single possible three-character .com domain (more than 50,000) has long since been registered.

The highest publicly reported amount of money paid for a domain name is $7.5 million in stock options, to buy business.com.

A single individual, Dr. Lieven P. Van Neste, reportedly owns more than 200,000 domain names.

The town of Halfway, Oregon, temporarily changed its name to Half.com as a publicity stunt for the website of the same name.

Scandinavia leads the world in Internet access, according to the United Nations' communications agency.

Twenty-seven percent of all web transactions are abandoned at the payment screen.

Four out of five visitors never come back to a website.

Space on a big company's homepage is worth about 1,300 times as much as land in the business districts of Tokyo.

SPAM A LOT

The time spent deleting spam emails costs U.S. businesses about $10 billion annually.

Spam filters that catch the word "Cialis" will not allow many work-related emails through because that word is embedded inside the word "specialist."

Replying more than one hundred times to the same piece of spam email will overwhelm the sender's system and interfere with their ability to send any more spam.

DEPARTMENT OF TRANSPORTATION

An X-ray security scanner that sees through people's clothes has been deployed at Heathrow Airport.

The cruise liner *Queen Elizabeth II* burns a gallon of diesel for every six inches that it moves.

An employee of the Alabama Department of Transportation installed spyware on his boss's computer and

proved that the boss spent 10 percent of his time working, 20 percent of his time checking stocks, and 70 percent of his time playing solitaire. The employee was fired,
but the boss kept his job.

> Monster truck engines are custom-built, alcohol-
> injected, and usually cost around $35,000. They
> burn 2 to 2.5 gallons of methanol per run (approxi-
> mately 250 feet).

Airbags inflate at a rate of 200 miles per hour.

> The air force's F-117 fighter uses aerodynamics dis-
> covered during research into how bumblebees fly.

INGENIOUS ENGINEERING

It took approximately 2.5 million stones to build the
Pyramid of Giza, the oldest and largest of the pyramids
on the Giza Plateau, and the only remaining Wonder of
the Ancient World. If you disassembled it, you would get
enough stones to encircle the earth with a brick wall
twenty inches high.

> The Netherlands has built 800 miles of massive dikes
> and seawalls to hold back the sea.

Humans have dammed up more than 10 trillion gallons
of water over the past four decades.

STORMY WEATHER

Some large clouds store enough water for 500,000 showers.

The world's windiest place is Commonwealth Bay, Antarctica. Winds regularly exceed 150 miles per hour.

The average diameter of a raindrop is 1 to 2 millimeters, and they fall from the sky on average 21 feet per second.

The animals most likely to fall from the sky during a rainstorm are fish and frogs. Occasionally the animals survive the fall. In 1894 jellyfish fell from the sky in Bath, England.

Lightning strikes the ground about six thousand times per minute.

Half of all forest fires are started by lightning.

It is thought that the sound of thunder is caused by the rapid expansion of the air surrounding the path of a lightning bolt.

MAN-MADE MESSES

Each year, 16 million gallons of oil run off pavements into streams, rivers, and eventually oceans in the United States. That is more oil than was spilled by the *Exxon Valdez*.

The rain in New York carries so much acid from pollution that it has killed all the fish in two hundred lakes in the Adirondack State Park.

Two to four million tons of oil leak into the water table every year from the Siberian pipeline.

WEIRD SCIENCE

Natural gas has no odor. The smell is added artificially so that leaks can be detected.

Siberia contains more than 25 percent of the world's forests.

The dioxin 2,3,7,8-tetrachlorodibenzo-p-dioxin is 150,000 times deadlier than cyanide.

The only rock that floats in water is pumice.

Electricity doesn't move through a wire but through a field around the wire.

PHYSICAL EDUCATION

Physicists have already performed a simple type of teleportation, transferring the quantum characteristics of one atom onto another atom at a different location.

The light from your computer monitor streams at you at almost 186,000 miles a second.

An ounce of gold can be stretched into a wire 50 miles long.

GOING THE DISTANCE

Sound carries so well in the Arctic that, on a calm day, a conversation can be heard from 1.8 miles away.

If you are standing on a mountaintop and the conditions are just right, you can see a lit match from 50 miles away.

If you were to count off 1 billion seconds, it would take you 31.7 years.

If Mount Everest were at the bottom of the ocean, its peak would be more than a mile underwater.

THE PLANET STRIKES BACK

In 1783, a volcanic eruption in Iceland threw up enough dust to temporarily block out the sun over Europe.

There is an average of two earthquakes every minute in the world.

After the Krakatoa volcano eruption in 1883 in Indonesia, many people reported that, because of the dust, the sunset appeared green and the moon blue.

A coal-mine fire in Haas Canyon, Colorado, was

ignited by spontaneous combustion in 1916 and withstood all efforts to put it out. The 900- to 1,700-degree fire was eventually quenched by heat-resistant foam mixed with grout in 2000.

An iceberg the size of Long Island once broke off Antarctica and blocked sea lanes used by both ships and penguins.

The winter of 1932 was so cold that Niagara Falls froze completely solid.

About 1 percent of the land area in the United States has been hit by tornadoes in the last century.

In 2003, there were eighty-six days of below-freezing weather in Hell, Michigan. However, residents (called "Hellions") determine whether Hell has "frozen over" by whether a certain dam stops flowing. This has only happened once so far, on January 24, 2004.

🐾 SHORT SHRIFT

The magnetic North Pole changes position by about twenty feet a day.

The Eiffel Tower shrinks six inches in winter.

Mexico City sinks about ten inches a year.

IN THE WILD

Orthodox rabbis warn that New York City drinking water might not be kosher; it contains harmless microorganisms that are technically shellfish.

A small child could crawl through a blue whale's major arteries.

Urea is found in mammalian and amphibian urine, as well as some fish, but not birds or reptiles.

FLORA FINDINGS

Plants that are not cared for will cry for help; a thirsty plant will make a high-pitched sound that is too high for humans to hear.

Six of the seven continents can grow pumpkins. Antarctica is the exception.

Plants can suffer from jet lag.

It can take up to fifteen years for a Christmas tree to grow, but on average, it takes about seven years.

The largest flower in the world is the *Rafflesia arnoldii*, which can grow to be three feet across and up to twenty-four pounds.

The smallest flower in the world is the water-meal,

which is only 1/42 of an inch long and 1/85 of an inch wide. It weighs approximately the same as two grains of salt.

CROWN JEWELS

The biggest natural crystals in the world are found in a silver mine in Mexico called the Cave of Crystals. They are made of gypsum, and some of them are 50 feet long.

The Cullinan Diamond is the largest gem-quality diamond ever discovered. Found in 1905, the original 3,100 carats were cut to make jewels for the British Crown Jewels and the British Royal Family's collection.

SNOWED UNDER

The large number of reflecting surfaces of the crystal makes snow appear white.

Sleet is a form of snow that begins to fall, but melts on its way down.

Partly melted ice crystals usually cling together to form snowflakes, which may in rare cases grow to three to four inches diameter in size.

A snowflake can take up to an hour to fall from the cloud to the surface of the Earth.

An iceberg weighs about 20 million tons on average.

It is estimated that 10,000,000,000,000,000,000,000,000,000,000,000,000 snowflakes have fallen to the Earth since it was formed.

In 1887, the largest snowflakes on record fell to the Earth in Montana. Each snowflake was 15 inches in diameter.

SURFACE TENSION

Twenty percent of the Earth's surface is permanently frozen.

In Gabon, there are several 1.8-billion-year-old natural nuclear reactors.

The Earth is turning to desert at a rate of 40 square miles per day.

The most abundant metal in the Earth's crust is aluminum.

THE OUTER LIMITS . . .

There are more stars than all of the grains of sand on Earth.

A solar day on the planet Mercury is twice as long as its year.

Due to gravitational effects, you weigh slightly less when the moon is directly overhead.

The planet Saturn has a density lower than water so, if there was a bathtub large enough to hold it, Saturn would float.

When you look at the full moon, what you see is only one-fifth the size of Africa.

The fastest shooting stars travel at 150,000 miles per hour.

It is impossible for a solar eclipse to last for more than seven minutes and forty seconds.

If the human body had the same mass as the sun, it would actually produce more heat.

Some asteroids in our solar system are so large that they even have their own moons.

Earth's warm summer and cold winter are not caused by varying distance from the sun, but rather by the tilt of the Earth's axis as its proceeds in its orbit.

🌰 SPACE RACE

The last time an astronaut walked on the moon was in 1979.

The first meal eaten on the moon by Neil Armstrong and Buzz Aldrin was four bacon squares, three sugar cookies, peaches, pineapple-grapefruit drink, and coffee.

The telescope on Mount Palomar, California, can see a distance of 7,038,835,200,000,000 million miles.

The Mars Rover *Spirit* is powered by six small motors the size of C batteries. It has a top speed of 0.1 miles per hour.

LET ME ENTERTAIN YOU

AWARDS NIGHT

Around 5,800 members of the Academy of Motion Picture Arts and Sciences vote for the Oscars.

The first Best Actor Oscar went to Emil Jannings in 1929 for his movies *The Way of All Flesh* and *The Last Command*. He didn't turn up to accept it.

The longest Oscars ceremony, in 2000, lasted a butt-numbing 256 minutes.

It takes twelve people twenty hours to make one Oscar statuette.

Three Oscars have been refused by winners, including Marlon Brando, who rejected his second Oscar, in 1972 for *The Godfather*.

Since 1950, neither winners nor heirs may sell the

statuette without offering to sell it back to the Academy first for $1.

When Orson Welles won the Best Screenplay Oscar for his classic *Citizen Kane* in 1941, it wasn't a popular choice. The audience booed.

Potential Oscar winners were told to keep acceptance speeches to forty-five seconds after Greer Garson's 1942 speech clocked in at five minutes and thirty seconds

In 1979, Oscar-winning actress Shirley MacLaine used the podium to cheer up her sibling, Warren Beatty, who had lost out for *Heaven Can Wait*. "I want to use this opportunity to say how proud I am of my little brother. Just imagine what you could accomplish if you tried celibacy!" He was not amused.

In 1938, Walt Disney won one full-sized Oscar and seven miniature Oscars for his classic *Snow White and the Seven Dwarfs*.

Cabaret star Liza Minnelli is the only Oscar winner with two Oscar-winning parents—her mom, Judy Garland, was a winner in 1939, and her dad, Vincente Minnelli, in 1958.

Titanic star Leonardo DiCaprio says he practiced his losing smile for the Oscars that year because he knew he wouldn't win the Best Actor trophy.

Denzel Washington and his wife, Pauletta, have a special trophy room in their California home to display all of their accolades. While Washington has won awards— including two Academy Awards—for his acting, his spouse has been honored many times over as a concert pianist.

The red carpet at the 2004 Grammy Awards was green because the event was sponsored by beer company Heineken.

Jennifer Aniston reportedly wore underwear with a picture of Brad Pitt on it to the 2003 Emmy Awards.

The Karl Lagerfeld–designed Chanel dress that Sarah Jessica Parker wore to the 2003 Emmy Awards took 250 hours to make.

SALARY DISPUTES

The average cost of making and marketing a major Hollywood movie in 2006 was $100.3 million.

The estates of twenty-two dead celebrities earned over $5 million in 2004. These celebrities include Elvis Presley, Dr. Seuss, Charles Schulz, J. R. R. Tolkien, and John Lennon.

Toto the dog was paid $125 per week while filming *The Wizard of Oz*.

The Swedish pop group ABBA once turned down an offer of $1 billion to reunite.

Supermodel Claudia Schiffer was paid £200,000 (about $400,000) to make a one-minute cameo in the film *Love Actually*.

Jerry Seinfeld once received approximately $600,000 for a fifteen-minute gig in Las Vegas.

Bruce Willis holds the record for the biggest payout for voice-over work, after receiving $10 million for 1990's *Look Who's Talking Too*.

Hotel heiress sisters Paris and Nicky Hilton are each expected to inherit $30 million.

To mark young actor Tyler Hoechlin's sixteenth birthday, Tom Hanks—who played his father in *Road to Perdition*—sent him $16.

Andie MacDowell worked at McDonald's and Pizza Hut as a teen.

Steve Martin once worked at Disneyland selling maps and guidebooks.

Sean "P. Diddy" Combs had his first job at age two when he modeled in an ad for Baskin-Robbins ice-cream shops.

Kevin Costner has twice taken on roles after Harrison Ford turned them down—Ford was the original choice to star in *Dragonfly* and *JFK*.

While attending the University of Iowa, Ashton Kutcher helped pay his tuition fees by sweeping floors at a local General Mills plant.

Everybody Loves Raymond star Patricia Heaton once worked as a morning room-service waitress at New York's Park Le Meridien hotel.

Madonna once worked as a coat-check girl at New York's Russian Tea Room restaurant, but she was fired for wearing fishnet stockings.

Oscar-winner Holly Hunter used to be a poultry judge in her native Georgia.

Billy Bob Thornton once spent eighteen months working in a Los Angeles pizza parlor. He was so good he worked his way up to assistant manager.

Playboy magnate Hugh Hefner auctioned off his address book containing the phone numbers of some of the most beautiful women in the world—along with memorabilia including portraits of Marilyn Monroe, Madonna, and Brigitte Bardot—to mark the fiftieth anniversary of the men's magazine.

SHOPPING SPREES

During a one-day shopping spree in Japan, Lil' Kim spent $50,000 on clothes—and Barbie dolls.

Vivica A. Fox once ruined a diamond-encrusted dress worth $1.5 million with red wine.

Nicole Richie has six pet rats and gave her *Simple Life* co-star Paris Hilton a rat she called Tori Spelling for Christmas.

50 Cent's $18.5 million mansion in Farmington, Connecticut, is the largest in the entire state. The pad used to belong to Mike Tyson and boasts eighteen bedrooms, thirty-eight bathrooms, and a man-made waterfall.

Eminem and 50 Cent had very simple backstage requests at the MTV Music Video Awards; while other stars were demanding bowls of raw vegetables and expensive alcohol, the rap pair asked for four boxes of Kentucky Fried Chicken and large portions of Mexican treats from Taco Bell.

Director Quentin Tarantino was so impressed with the bar from the fictitious House of Blue Leaves, created for his movie *Kill Bill*, he had it installed in his Hollywood home.

Celebrity parents Will Smith, Madonna, Chris O'Donnell,

and Kevin Kline are among the many stars who have splurged on Posh Tots' mini mansions, castles, and chalets for their children to play in. The prices for the little homes range from $2,700 to $100,000.

George Clooney bought a couple of *Charlie's Angels* star Lucy Liu's arty collages when she had a brief stint with him on *ER*.

Lil' Kim's manicurist charged up to $6,300 a day to wrap her nails in shredded $100 bills.

Roc-A-Fella hip-hop mogul Damon Dash—who owns more than three thousand pairs of sneakers—never wears the same clothes twice and refuses to write in red ink because it signifies losing money.

Cameron Diaz insists on being environmentally friendly even when she's being ferried to awards shows and events—she uses Los Angeles's Evo Limo Luxury Car Service, where all vehicles run on natural gas.

The first thing Keira Knightley bought with her first movie paycheck was a doll's house.

Renée Zellweger carries two cell phones around with her— one for calls from England and the other for American calls.

Oprah Winfrey sleeps on Frette bedsheets, which boast a very high thread count and sell for up to $3,000 a set.

Troubled singer Michael Jackson once paid $30,000 to hire two private jets—one for him to travel in and another as a decoy to confuse the press when he traveled from Las Vegas, Nevada, to Santa Barbara, California.

> One Christmas, *Friends* stars Jennifer Aniston, Courteney Cox, Lisa Kudrow, Matt LeBlanc, Matthew Perry, and David Schwimmer gave plasma TVs to crew members who'd worked on the show for less than five years—while those who'd passed the five-year mark received Mini Cooper cars.

FAMILY CONNECTIONS

A genealogist once claimed to have proof that Oprah Winfrey and Elvis Presley are distant cousins.

> Keanu Reeves's father has served time in prison for heroin possession.

Woody Harrelson's father was a hitman convicted of assassinating a federal judge.

> Edward Norton's grandfather designed the city of Columbia, Maryland, where Norton grew up. He also helped develop Baltimore's Inner Harbor, Norfolk's Waterside Festival Marketplace, and Boston's Quincy Market,

Julianna Margulies's father wrote the "Plop-Plop, Fizz-Fizz" Alka-Seltzer commercial.

David Hasselhoff's great-uncle was Karl Hasselhoff, the inventor of inflatable sheep.

Coldplay like to keep in touch with their family and friends when they're touring—their backstage requirements include eight stamped, local postcards.

Kevin Spacey's older brother is a professional Rod Stewart impersonator.

Steven Spielberg is Drew Barrymore's godfather. After seeing her nude in *Playboy* magazine, he sent her a blanket with a note telling her to cover herself up.

Catherine Zeta-Jones's son Dylan has become so close to his mother's pal George Clooney that he now refers to the actor as Uncle George.

Eminem's parents once fronted a cover group called Daddy Warbucks.

Uma Thurman carried home rocks from the different locations where she filmed *Kill Bill* for her children, Maya and Roan.

Dave Matthews and his wife, Ashley, have matching wedding bands made out of pressed pennies from the years they were born, 1967 and 1973.

Athens-born rocker Tommy Lee's mother was Miss Greece in 1957.

Actress Daryl Hannah's brother is a skydiving instructor.

Jack Osbourne had "Mum" tattooed in a heart on his left shoulder as a special thank-you to mom Sharon, who helped him battle his drug- and alcohol-abuse problems.

Duran Duran frontman Simon Le Bon has historical controversy in his past—he can trace his family tree back to Europe's Huguenots, who were forced to find refuge in England after being chased out of France by the Catholics for their Protestant beliefs.

Brooke Shields can trace her heritage back to famous historical figures like Charlemagne and Lucrezia Borgia.

Three generations of the Astin family have acted in director Peter Jackson's films. Sean Astin played Samwise Gamgee in the *Lord of the Rings* trilogy; his young daughter, Ali, played his child in *The Return of the King*; and his dad, John Astin, appeared in Jackson's 1996 movie *The Frighteners*.

Harrison Ford is so in love with his fiancée, Calista Flockhart, that he drinks out of a cup decorated with their pictures and names.

Patrick Presley, a cousin of rock legend Elvis, hanged himself while in jail in Mississippi over a fatal car accident.

Mike Myers's wedding ring is his late father's 1956 Encyclopedia Britannica Salesman of the Year gift.

Kiefer Sutherland has his family's Scottish crest tattooed on his back. It's one of six tattoos the actor boasts.

SIX DEGREES OF SEPARATION

Demi Moore and Ashton Kutcher spent the Halloween of 2003 dressed as rival supercouple Jennifer Lopez and Ben Affleck.

Sting is Leonardo DiCaprio's next-door neighbor in Malibu, California.

Patrick Swayze's first crush was on a dancer his mother taught, named Ellen Smith. The young girl later changed her name to Jaclyn Smyth and became an original Charlie's Angel.

Kate Winslet gave birth to her son Joe with the music of Rufus Wainwright in the background.

Kathy Hilton, mother of hotel heiress Paris Hilton, went to school with pop singer Janet Jackson.

Sophia Loren, Liz Taylor, and Raquel Welch were all considered for the role of *Dynasty* TV bitch Alexis before Joan Collins landed the part.

Ellen Degeneres and Harry Connick Jr.'s fathers worked on a paper route together as children in their native New Orleans, Louisiana.

Cher turned down Geena Davis's role in *Thelma & Louise.*

Ozzy Osbourne and opera singer Sarah Brightman used to go to the same vocal coach in London.

Eminem and Wyclef Jean are the same age; both were born on October 17, 1972.

Jim Carrey, Ellen Degeneres, and *Frasier* star Jane Leeves were in the same acting class before hitting fame.

Ray Romano went to high school with actress Fran Drescher.

Prince Charles sent a bottle of whiskey to recovering alcoholic Ozzy Osbourne after his bike crash.

Lenny Kravitz kept a marijuana joint he'd shared with Rolling Stone Mick Jagger for a year as a tribute.

In 1977, the legendary Groucho Marx died three days after Elvis Presley died. Unfortunately, due to the fevered commotion caused by Presley's unanticipated death, the media paid little attention to the passing of the brilliant comic.

The trucking company Elvis Presley worked at as a young man was owned by Frank Sinatra.

"WARS" WISDOM

For *Star Wars*'s twentieth anniversary, the first episode film renovation cost as much as the original movie.

During *The Empire Strikes Back*'s famous asteroid scene, one of the deadly hurling asteroids is actually a potato.

The sound effect for the light sabers was recorded by moving a microphone next to a television set.

The Strokes star Nikolai Fraiture once shamed his dad when he was caught trying to steal a Luke Sky-walker doll from the Macy's store where his father worked as a security guard.

In the opening scene of *Raiders of the Lost Ark*, Indy escapes with the golden idol in a seaplane with the registration number OB-3PO. This, of course, refers to Obi-Wan and C-3PO.

It only took legendary actor Alec Guinness six hours to film all his scenes for *The Empire Strikes Back*.

Return of the Jedi was originally titled *Revenge of the Jedi*—but later underwent a title change because, according to director George Lucas, a Jedi would never take revenge.

Sections of the under-construction *Death Star* in *Return of the Jedi* resemble the San Francisco skyline, the silhouette of a favorite city of George Lucas.

A small pair of metal dice can be seen hanging in the *Millennium Falcon*'s cockpit as Chewbacca prepares to depart from Mos Eisley. The dice do not appear in subsequent scenes.

Chewbacca's name is inspired by the name of Chebika

City, in Tunisia, near the place where Tatooine scenes in *Star Wars* were shot.

The *Millennium Falcon*'s design was originally inspired by the shape of a hamburger with an olive on the side.

Jodie Foster was George Lucas's second choice to play the part of Princess Leia.

The name of 4-LOM, one the bounty hunters listening to Darth Vader in *The Empire Strikes Back*, means: For Love of Money.

In 1996, 37 percent of the toys sold in the United States were Star Wars products.

STARS STRUCK

Paul Newman is color-blind.

Sandra Bullock is allergic to horses.

Lara Flynn Boyle is dyslexic.

Mike Myers has an aversion to being touched.

Johnny Depp is afraid of clowns.

Two of Ashton Kutcher's toes on his right foot are webbed.

Sandra Bullock has revealed she uses hemorrhoid cream on her face.

Accident-prone Orlando Bloom has broken his skull three times, both legs, a finger, a toe, a rib, an arm, a wrist, his nose, and his back.

While on a training schedule and drinking protein drinks to enhance her muscles, Halle Berry confessed she couldn't stop breaking wind as a result of the drinks.

In 2004, David Bowie thought he was being stalked by someone dressed as a giant pink rabbit. Bowie noticed the fan at several concerts, but he became alarmed when he got on a plane and the bunny was on board.

Pamela Anderson failed her first driving test when she hit another car. She passed on her fourth attempt.

Former TV Superman Dean Cain was a onetime football star in Buffalo, New York. The actor signed on with the Buffalo Bills after leaving Princeton University but seriously injured his knee and had to retire before he had played a game for the team.

MUSICAL STYLINGS

The song "When Irish Eyes Are Smiling" was written by George Graff and Chauncey Olcott and composed by Ernest Ball; all three were Americans and reportedly had never visited Ireland.

Ozzy Osbourne has two smiley-face tattoos etched on his kneecaps so he can talk to them when he's feeling lonely.

Janet Jackson's "wardrobe malfunction" at the 2004 Super Bowl has become the most searched for event in the history of the Internet. Viacom, which at the time owned broadcaster CBS, was fined $550,000. This could be paid with only 7.5 seconds of commercial time during the same Super Bowl telecast.

Jessica Simpson used to keep photographs of missing children under her pillow and pray for them every night when she was a teenager. She also wanted to adopt a Mexican baby from an orphanage she visited when she was sixteen.

Clay Aiken is allergic to mushrooms, shellfish, chocolate, mint, and coffee.

Eminem's two favorite places to tour are Amsterdam, because of its liberal laws, and London, because of its food.

Harry Connick Jr. quit smoking when his idol Mel Torme told him he'd never speak to him again until he was nicotine-free.

Soul-star-turned-reverend Al Green was so worried about including words like "baby" and "sugar" in songs on his album *I Can't Stop* that he asked for guidance from the congregation at his Tennessee church.

Spanish crooner Julio Iglesias holds the record for selling more albums in more languages than any other singer.

Tupac Shakur came up with his signature shaven hairstyle because he suffered from premature baldness.

Former Destiny's Child singer Farrah Franklin's middle name is Destiny.

Robbie Williams once posed as a beggar in Times Square and gave $100 to the first person who gave him money.

Madonna likes to sing "Truly Scrumptious" from hit musical *Chitty Chitty Bang Bang* to her children.

San Francisco–based Neil Diamond tribute group Super Diamond are the world's top cover band—they charge $20,000 per show.

Beyoncé Knowles's hit single "Crazy in Love" was the bestselling cell-phone ring tone in Britain in 2003.

U2 uses a sound system on tour that weighs thirty tons.

Justin Timberlake's 2003 Christmas show in Dublin, Ireland, sold out in forty seconds.

Justin Timberlake was so impressed by Queen's "Bohemian Rhapsody" as a child that he locked himself away in his bedroom for two days straight to listen to the track over and over again.

Pink has a ritual every time she releases a new album—she takes a bottle of champagne to New York's Virgin Megastore and buys the first copy.

Bryan Adams's song "Everything I Do (I Do It for You)" is the track most couples pick for the first dance at their weddings.

🌰 TWO LEFT FEET

In 1912, the Archbishop of Paris declared dancing the tango a sin.

The Mexican Hat Dance or *Jarabe tapatío* is the official dance of Mexico.

Professional ballerinas use about twelve pairs of toe shoes per week.

Billy Idol has revealed he shaves his gray pubic hair.

Macy Gray once stunned fans by performing naked on stage—except for a pair of designer shoes.

Barbra Streisand insisted on spraying her black microphone white for her performance on *The Oprah Winfrey Show* so it matched her off-white outfit.

American Idol bosses banned wannabe pop stars from

singing Alicia Keys's "Fallin'" in tryouts, because judges Simon Cowell, Randy Jackson, and Paula Abdul grew tired of the song.

Bruce Springsteen's triumphant concert at Boston's Fenway Park on September 6, 2003, was the first rock show in the baseball stadium's ninety-one-year history.

Rapper NAS's thirtieth birthday cake was iced with green marijuana leaves, as a nod to his hemp advocacy.

Thousands of Britons say they would like Robbie Williams's song "Angels" played at their funeral.

A schoolgirl once asked band Coldplay for their autographs to sell for charity—and got a triple platinum disc worth $8,000.

Kelsey Grammer performed the *Frasier* theme song.

Jonathan Davis, lead singer of Korn, played in his high school bagpipe band.

"Rudolph the Red-Nosed Reindeer" was created in 1939 in Chicago for the Montgomery Ward department stores for a Christmas promotion. The words were originally the poem "Rollo, the red-nosed reindeer" by Robert L. May. Montgomery Ward liked it but didn't like the name Rollo so they changed it to Rudolph. It wasn't set to music until 1947, and Gene Autry recorded the hit song in 1949.

BEATLEMANIA

Throughout their career, the Beatles spent more than four hundred weeks on the music charts.

During the recording of "Hey Jude," Ringo Starr left the room to use the bathroom and almost missed his drum cue.

Only 6 percent of the Beatles's autographs in circulation are estimated to be real.

John Lennon was expelled from school for misbehavior at age five.

In the '60s, Paul McCartney had three cats named Jesus, Mary, and Joseph.

John Lennon's mother taught him how to play an old Spanish guitar like a banjo. His mother died after being hit by a car.

Paul McCartney used the working words "scrambled eggs" before coming up with "yesterday" while composing that song.

Ringo Starr cannot swim, except for a brief doggie paddle.

John Lennon was raised by his mother's sister, Mimi Smith.

Manager Brian Epstein made the Beatles cut their hair short after he signed them in 1962.

By age fifteen, John Lennon was a big fan of Elvis.

In 1965, John Lennon's dad, Alfred, made a record called "That's My Life."

It has been reported that John Lennon got a big thrill out of shoplifting when he was young.

George Harrison was afraid of flying.

An American firm wrote to the Beatles asking if they could market the Beatles's bathwater at a dollar a bottle. They refused the offer.

John Lennon had dyslexia.

Ringo Starr received far more fan mail than any of the other Beatles.

"Lovely Rita Meter Maid" was inspired by Paul McCartney's parking ticket from a female warden on Abbey Road in London.

In 1996, Ringo Starr appeared in a Japanese advertisement for apple sauce, which coincidentally is what "ringo" means in Japanese.

John Lennon named his band the Beatles after Buddy Holly's Crickets.

Paul McCartney was regularly the first Beatle dressed for performances.

Without glasses, John Lennon was legally blind.

At the end of "A Day in the Life," an ultrasonic whistle, audible only to dogs, sounds.

John Lennon's favorite food was cornflakes.

Paul McCartney and Pete Best were once arrested in Hamburg because they stuck a condom to the wall and set it on fire.

POP CULTURE TIDBITS

Bill Murray doesn't have a publicist or an agent.

Nicole Kidman has said that when she was younger she used to pray she would be turned into a witch.

Mike Myers has two streets named after him in his native Toronto.

Jennifer Aniston ate the same lunch—consisting of lettuce, garbanzo beans, turkey, and lemon dressing—every day for nine years.

Tom Cruise had attended fifteen schools by the time he was fourteen.

Screenwriter and director Quentin Tarantino wrote a script called "Captain Peachfuzz and the Anchovy Bandit" as a child.

The original title of cult TV show *Charlie's Angels* was *Alleycats*.

Halle Berry's stint on *Saturday Night Live* was so chaotic that she appeared for the final curtain call with her boots on the wrong feet.

Hollywood legend Zsa Zsa Gábor hosted the Rubik's Cube's launch in America, beginning with a Hollywood party on May 5, 1980.

During eight years of *Seinfeld*, Cosmo Kramer went through Jerry Seinfeld's apartment door 284 times.

Elizabeth Hurley has twelve piercings in her ears and a pierced nose.

In all three *Godfather* films, when you see oranges, there is a death (or a very close call) coming up soon.

Malnourished magician David Blaine's first public meal after his self-imposed forty-four-day incarceration in a plastic box suspended over London's River Thames was a plate of chicken satay at Mr. Chow's restaurant.

He followed this with a big helping of dessert. He opted to fast for forty-four days because the number correlates with his birthday, April 4.

Dennis Rodman claims the police have visited his Newport Beach, California, home more than eighty times because of noise complaints. Dennis Rodman also claims he has pierced his penis three times.

Prince Charles has launched his own range of shampoos and conditioners under his company Duchy Originals.

FANTASY FACTS

Donald Duck lives at 1313 Webfoot Walk, Duckburg, Calisota.

It is believed that in early versions of the Cinderella story, her famous slippers were originally made out of fur. The glass slipper is unique to the 1697 Charles Perrault version, which is the most popular. In the classic Disney animated movie, it was the left shoe that Cinderella lost at the stairway, when the prince tried to follow her.

Pinocchio was made of pine—the name means "pine eye," the Tuscan term for a pine nut.

Winnie-the-Pooh author A. A. Milne's full name is Alan Alexander Milne.

When the decision was made in 1962 that cartoon family the Flintstones would have a baby, the child was going to be a boy. Later, they decided that a girl would make for better merchandising, such as dolls.

Disney's *The Lion King* has become the most successful DVD re-release ever, after 3 million copies of the new DVD sold in two days.

An alternative title for sitcom *Friends* was *Insomnia Café*.

Oprah Winfrey says her two favorite interviews of all time were with Sidney Poitier and Salma Hayek.

Ben Affleck appeared in a one-line role playing a basketball player in the 1992 film *Buffy the Vampire Slayer*.

Bill Murray co-owns a minor-league baseball team in St. Paul, Minnesota, called the St. Paul Saints.

Jim Carrey voted in 2004 at the Beverly Hills City Hall. He had an assistant wait in line for him, however.

Zeppo Marx invented a wristwatch that would monitor the heart rate of cardiac patients and sound an alarm if they went into cardiac arrest.

The movie *Monty Python's Life of Brian* was banned in several countries upon its release, including Ireland and Norway.

Robert De Niro played the part of the Cowardly Lion in his elementary school's production of *The Wizard of Oz*. De Niro was ten at the time.

HAL in *2001: Space Odyssey* is an abbreviation for "Heuristically programmed ALgorithmic computer."

Napoleon Bonaparte is the historical figure most often portrayed in movies. He has been featured in 194 movies, while Jesus Christ has featured in 152 and Abraham Lincoln in 137.

David Letterman was voted Class Smart Aleck at his hometown high school, Broad Ripple High.

Lisa Kudrow has a degree in biology from Vassar College.

In the film *Forrest Gump*, all the still photos show Forrest with his eyes closed.

The director of the 2005 version of *Charlie and the Chocolate Factory*, Tim Burton, spent millions training squirrels to crack nuts to re-create the Nut Room scene.

It was illegal to sell E.T. dolls in France because there is a law against selling dolls without human faces.

FRISKY BUSINESS

CONSUMER REPORTS

In a recent poll, 23 percent of workers said they would work harder if their employer offered a $1,000 shopping spree at a store of their choice.

The busiest shopping hour of the Christmas season is between 3 p.m. and 4 p.m. on Christmas Eve.

The average child recognizes more than two hundred company logos by the time he enters elementary school.

Five years ago, 60 percent of all retail purchases were made with cash or check. Now it's 50 percent. By 2010, only 39 percent of purchases will be made by cash or check.

One in four homeless people in South Korea has a credit card.

Grocery shoppers spend an average of eight minutes waiting in line at the supermarket.

A woman who went shopping at a store in Britain once found $30,000 in cash on the floor near a checkout.

GOING ONCE, GOING TWICE . . .

There are approximately 18 million items for sale at any given moment on eBay.

There are $680 worth of eBay transactions each second.

A Scud missile complete with its own launcher truck has been up for sale on eBay.

SWEDISH MEATBALLS

One in ten Europeans was conceived on an Ikea bed, according to the company.

More copies of the Ikea catalog are printed each year than the Bible.

Ikea once apologized after accidentally naming a child's bunk bed similarly to an obscene German expression. The wooden bed was called the "Gutvik," which if pronounced a certain way sounds like "gut fick," which means "good fuck" in German.

PEDAL TO THE METAL

Draftsmen make about 27,000 drawings for the manufacturing of a new car.

At General Motors, the cost of health care for employees now exceeds the cost of steel for cars.

The average car in Japan is driven 4,400 miles per year. In the United States, the average is 8,200 miles per year.

The Malaysian government has banned car commercials featuring Brad Pitt because they are "an insult to Asians."

A man who began working for a Ford dealership in England in 1930 was still working there at the age of ninety-two.

HUMBLE ORIGINS

First-year sales of famous products:
  VW Beetle: 330
  Wite-Out: 1,200 bottles
  Cuisinart food processor: 200
  Remington typewriter: 8
  Scrabble: 532
  Coca-Cola: 25 bottles

Procter & Gamble originally manufactured candles before moving on to soap.

Dr. George F. Grant received U.S. patent number 638,920 on December 12, 1899, for his invention—the golf tee. He created it because he didn't want to get his hands dirty by building a mound of dirt to place his ball on.

In 1810, Peter Durand invented the tin can for preserving food.

In 1789, Dr. Guillotin merely proposed the machine that bears his name, and he never made a working model. In fact, he was opposed to the death penalty. The first working model was made by his assistant years later. When the machine attained infamy during the French Revolution, Dr. Guillotin protested its use and went to his grave claiming that the machine was unjustly named after him.

The drink Gatorade was named after the University of Florida Gators and was first developed at that school.

George Eastman, inventor of the Kodak camera, hated having his picture taken.

David McConnell started the California Perfume Company in 1886 after selling his own homemade perfumes along with books door-to-door and discovering that the perfumes were much more popular. Today the company is known as Avon.

MAIL PATTERN ODDNESS

The U.S. Postal Service owns 176,000 cars and trucks, the largest civilian vehicle fleet on Earth.

The Royal Mail in Britain once launched a search for

the owner of a set of traffic lights sent through the mail.

The Belgians have tried to deliver mail using cats. It didn't work.

There has been no mail delivery in Canada on Saturday for the last thirty-five years.

A Chilean woman was horrified when she received a box through the post with a human brain inside it.

Mailmen in Russia now carry revolvers after a recent decision by the government.

A New Zealand town once produced its own postage stamp, but put the sticky part on the wrong side.

Post office staff in Malaysia once found 21,000 undelivered letters stored in an apartment that used to be rented out by one of their colleagues.

DOUBLE VENTI MOCHA CHAI LATTE WITH SOY MILK, PLEASE!

The first Starbucks opened in Seattle in 1971 at 2000 Western Avenue, across from the historic Pike Place Market.

Howard Schultz, the high-profile CEO of Starbucks, was *not* one of the three original founders. They were Jerry Baldwin, Zev Siegel, and Gordon Bowker.

There is a Starbucks in Myungdong, South Korea, that is five stories tall.

The Starbucks at the highest elevation is on Main Street in Breckenridge, Colorado.

9 TO 5

American office workers send an average of thirty-six emails per day.

Fifty-three percent of Americans think they are paid the right salary.

Twelve percent of businessmen wear their ties so tight that they restrict the blood flow to their brains.

One in six employees says he has gotten so mad at a coworker that he "felt like hitting them but didn't."

One in seven workers needs help turning his office computer on or off because of his dismal knowledge of new technology.

A Swedish man was awarded over $100,000 in compensation after he was fired for telling off a colleague for breaking wind.

One in three workers has come close to leaving his job because of the irritating habits of his colleagues, according to a survey.

SEX SELLS

A courier firm in Germany almost went bankrupt after an employee ran up a $40,000 cell phone bill by calling sex hotlines.

> Viagra became the top-selling medicine in Venezuela during the country's two-month general strike.

A British sex shop had to change an advertisement after council officials objected to the use of the word "gadget."

> Prostitution is legal in Germany; however, income from prostitution is taxed at a slightly higher rate than income from other occupations.

A Romanian taxi driver says his business has swelled since he started playing pornographic films in his cab for customers.

> A Danish company has given its employees free subscriptions to Internet pornography sites.

THE UNDERWEAR ECONOMY

According to market-research firm NPD Fashionworld, 50 percent of all lingerie purchases are returned to the store.

The world's first bra made completely of chocolate has gone on sale in Austria.

A lingerie designer has created a matching bra and panties out of human hair and is selling them for $5,000 a set.

THE WEIRD, THE STRANGE, AND THE PUZZLING

An Indian city is dumping garbage outside businesses that don't pay their taxes, to try to get them to pay up.

A German firm is printing novels on rolls of toilet paper to "kill two birds with one stone."

The Chinese airline Sichuan Airlines has paid $300,000 for the phone number 888-8888, saying it hopes to make its customers happy because eight is a lucky number in China. The phone number 666-6666 was sold for $2.75 million to a buyer in Qatar in 2006.

A German gas station is employing topless assistants in an attempt to boost trade.

A school has been set up in Italy to teach people how to become drag queens.

A struggling teashop owner in China lured customers by placing singles advertisements seeking a lover and then fixing the rendezvous in her café.

A company manufacturing skin cream from snail extract is exporting 20,000 bottles to the United States every month.

A Serbian tie maker is planning to launch a new range of penis cravats for the man who has everything.

THE AIR UP THERE

A Colombian airline has promised free flights for life to a baby born on board one of its planes.

The first in-flight movie was shown on April 6, 1925; it was a silent film on a Deutsche Lufthansa flight.

In 2004, Virgin Atlantic Airlines introduced a double bed for first-class passengers who fly together.

The first naked flight in 2003 carried eighty-seven passengers from Miami, Florida, to Cancún, Mexico.

Bodily Functions

HEAR NO EVIL . . .

There are nine muscles in the human ear.

The screaming of an upset baby can damage hearing. Kids can scream at levels up to 90 decibels, and permanent damage can be caused at 85 decibels.

Cerumen is the medical term for earwax. The ears secrete more earwax when you are afraid than when you aren't.

It only takes seven pounds of pressure to rip off an ear.

Wearing headphones for just one hour will multiply the number of bacteria in the ear 700 times.

SEE NO EVIL . . .

About one-third of the human race has twenty-twenty vision.

The human eye blinks an average of 4.2 million

times a year. A blink lasts approximately 300 to 400 milliseconds.

When you are looking at someone you love, your pupils dilate; they do the same when you are looking at someone you hate.

The number one cause of blindness in the United States is diabetes.

It is already known that Viagra can cause a form of temporary color-blindness. But recent evidence indicates that for some people it might also be the cause of what are essentially strokes in the eyes, causing permanent damage to optic nerves and thus permanent loss of vision.

SPEAK NO EVIL . . .

Approximately 55 percent of people yawn within five minutes of seeing someone else yawn. Reading about yawning makes most people yawn.

The average life span of a taste bud is ten days.

It takes food seven seconds to get from the mouth to the stomach.

During a kiss, as many as 278 bacteria colonies are exchanged.

Men get hiccups more often than women do.

A man named Charles Osborne had the hiccups for sixty-eight years.

Teeth normally start to appear six months after birth although some babies are born with neonatal teeth.

SNEEZE NO EVIL?

If you sneeze too hard, you can fracture a rib. If you try to suppress a sneeze, you can rupture a blood vessel in your head or neck and die.

The longest recorded sneezing fit lasted 978 days.

Humans can only smell one-twentieth as well as a dog.

The average American kid catches six colds a year; the average kid in daycare catches ten.

BABY BOOM

At the moment of conception, a fetus spends about half an hour as a single cell.

The three things pregnant women dream most of during their first trimester are frogs, worms, and potted plants.

Fetuses can hiccup.

Everyone is color-blind at birth.

TRICKY TREATMENTS

From 1898 to 1910, the German pharmaceutical company Bayer advertised heroin as cough medicine for children and a non-addictive morphine substitute to cure morphine addiction. Eventually it was discovered that heroin is actually converted to morphine when metabolized in the liver, leading the company to discontinue their marketing. Bayer lost trademark rights to heroin after World War I.

An eighty-year-old London woman had a gallstone removed that weighed 13 pounds 14 ounces.

Seventeenth-century hangover cures included flogging and bleeding by leeches.

The first successful open heart surgery was performed in 1896.

Breast reduction is the most common plastic surgery performed on American men.

Some arthritis medicine contains gold salts, which are used as an anti-inflammatory.

In the 1800s, people believed that gin could cure stomach problems.

The earliest form of electric shock treatment involved electric eels.

In medieval Japan, dentists extracted teeth with their hands.

Mark Twain thought fasting was a cure for illness. He would cure his colds and fevers by not eating for one or two days.

Ancient Egyptians believed eating fried mice would cure a toothache.

One of the first anesthetics was used to help surgeons, not patients. It was developed by the Ancient Incas of Peru more than a thousand years ago. While they worked, Inca surgeons chewed leaves of the coca plant to calm their nerves. We now know these leaves contain a powerful painkilling drug.

A Massachusetts surgeon once left a patient with an open incision for thirty-five minutes while he went to deposit a check.

Every year, 2,700 surgical patients go home from the hospital with metal tools, sponges, and other objects left inside them. In 2000, fifty-seven people died as a result of these mistakes.

The United States tops the world in plastic-surgery procedures. Second is Mexico.

Barbers at one time combined shaving and haircutting with bloodletting and pulling teeth.

The white stripes on a field of red that spiral down a barber pole represent the bandages once used in the bloodletting.

In about two out of a thousand cases where a patient is anesthetized, the patient will awaken and be mentally alert and feel all the pain of the surgery, but be paralyzed and unable to signal or communicate with the doctors.

Of all the medicines available on the international market today, 7 percent are fake. In some countries, the figure for counterfeit medicines can be as high as 50 percent.

LAWS OF AVERAGES

In 1991, the average bra size in the United States was 34B. Today it's 36C.

The average North Korean seven-year-old is almost three inches shorter than the average South Korean seven-year-old.

The average woman is five inches shorter than the average man.

The average human dream lasts two to three seconds.

INTERNAL AFFAIRS

Experts say the human body has 60,000 miles of blood vessels.

Your brain uses 40 percent of the oxygen that enters your bloodstream.

Blood plasma is about 92 percent water.

Sunburn seems to heal in just a few days, but the blood vessels under the skin do not return to their normal condition for up to fifteen months.

The stomach has 35 million digestive glands.

Side by side, two thousand cells from the human body could cover about one square inch.

The body contains about four ounces of salt.

If you calculated the length of a strand of DNA for one person, it would stretch across the diameter of the solar system.

The average heart beats 2.5 billion times in a lifetime. The heart beats about 100,000 times each day.

After drinking, the last place in the body to be cleared of alcohol is the brain.

Even mild dehydration will slow down one's metabolism as much as 3 percent.

The body gives off enough heat in thirty minutes to bring half a gallon of water to a boil.

The body uses more than seventy muscles to say one word and three hundred muscles to balance itself when standing still.

Bone is stronger, inch for inch, than the steel in skyscrapers.

Living brain cells are bright pink.

The body contains the same amount of iron as an iron nail.

It takes about twenty seconds for a red blood cell to circle the whole body.

Humans are born with 300 bones but, by the time they reach adulthood, they only have 206.

The right lung in humans is slightly larger than the left. The total surface area of a pair of human lungs is equal to that of a tennis court.

The attachment of human muscles to skin is what causes dimples.

A woman's heart beats faster than a man's does.

Dogs and humans are the only animals with prostates.

Human thighbones are stronger than concrete.

🌰 GETTING PHYSICAL

It takes twice as long to lose new muscle if you stop working out as it did to gain it.

The Amish diet is high in meat, dairy, refined sugars, and calories. Yet obesity is virtually unknown among them. The difference is, since they have no TVs, cars, or powered machines, they spend most of their time doing manual labor.

A runner consumes about seven quarts of oxygen while running a 100-yard dash.

You would have to walk 50 miles for your legs to equal the amount of exercise your eyes get daily.

Fidgeting can burn about 350 calories a day.

THIRSTING FOR KNOWLEDGE

The body loses half a liter of water a day through breathing.

In 37 percent of Americans, the thirst mechanism is so weak that it is often mistaken for hunger.

Seventy-five percent of Americans are chronically dehydrated.

A mere 2 percent drop in body water can trigger fuzzy short-term memory, trouble with basic math, and difficulty focusing on the computer screen or on a printed page.

In a hot climate, you can sweat as much as three gallons of water a day.

GIVING THE FINGER

The left hand performs an average of 56 percent of your typing.

Twelve percent of the British population is left-handed.

Injured fingernails grow faster than uninjured ones.

Fingernails are made from the same substance as a bird's beak.

BEST FOOT FORWARD

A pair of human feet contains 250,000 sweat glands. There are about 1 trillion bacteria on each foot.

The big toes have two bones each while the rest have three.

A shank is the part of the sole between the heel and the ball of the foot.

The talus is the second largest bone in the foot.

A thirteen-year-old child found a tooth growing out of his foot in 1977.

A HAIRY SITUATION

If the average male never shaved, his beard would be 13 feet long when he died.

Men without hair on their chests are more likely to get cirrhosis of the liver than men with hair.

An average human loses about two hundred head hairs per day.

KING OF PAIN

The most common phobia in the world is algophobia, which is the fear of pain.

Pain is measured in units of dols. The instrument used to measure pain is a dolorimeter.

SMOKE SCREEN

In a 1930 Quebec Junior Amateur game, hockey goalie Abie Goldberry was hit by a flying puck that ignited a pack of matches in his pocket, setting his uniform on fire. He was badly burned before his teammates could put the fire out.

Secondhand smoke contains more than four thousand chemicals including more than forty cancer-causing compounds. It contains twice as much tar and nicotine per unit volume as does smoke inhaled from a cigarette; three times as much cancer-causing benzopyrene; five times as much carbon monoxide; and fifty times as much ammonia.

Secondhand smoke from pipes and cigars is equally as harmful as the smoke from cigarettes, if not more so.

A HISTORY OF VIOLENCE

In 1992, 5,840 people checked into emergency rooms with "pillow-related injuries" and 2,421 people checked in with injuries involving houseplants.

In 1994, there were more than 420,000 accidents caused by kitchen knives, 122,000 by drinking glasses, 29,000 by refrigerators, and 7,000 by dishwashers.

A study published in a 1995 issue of the *Journal of Urology* estimated that 600,000 men in the United States are impotent from injuries to their crotches, about 40 percent of them from too-vigorous bicycling.

About eight thousand Americans are injured by musical instruments each year.

More than 90 percent of diseases are caused or complicated by stress.

The oldest-known disease in the world is leprosy.

In the summer of 1998, 470 Chinese people were injured by spontaneously exploding beer bottles.

Despite the large rat population in New York City, rats bite only 311 people in an average year. But 1,519 residents are bitten annually by other New Yorkers.

The two steps at the top and the two at the bottom are the four most dangerous steps in a staircase.

More than 11,000 people are injured every year trying out new sexual positions.

In the United States, 55,700 people are injured by jewelry each year.

On an average day in the United States, about forty people are hurt on trampolines.

Once a person is totally buried by an avalanche, there is only a one-in-three chance of survival.

Three hundred people report to emergency rooms across the country every day due to Rollerblading accidents.

Every year, more than 8,800 people injure themselves with a toothpick.

Lead poisoning was common among upper-class

Romans who used lead-sweetened wine and leaded grape pulp as a condiment.

More than 2,500 left-handed people are killed each year because they used products made for right-handed people.

According to the U.S. Department of Transportation, an average of 550 sleep-related highway accidents occur per day.

Nearly 60 percent of accidents involving pedestrians younger than five happen in their own driveway when a vehicle backs over them.

INTERNATIONAL INCIDENTS

An Austrian woman who hid behind her boyfriend's truck so that she could jump out and surprise him was taken to the hospital after he reversed over her.

An Ohio student hurt his head when a train struck him. He told police he was trying to see how close to the moving train he could place his head without getting hit.

A Thai man who held the record for spending time with snakes died after being bitten by a mamba.

An eighty-three-year-old Canadian woman was rescued after spending two days wedged behind her toilet.

A British woman came home to find her husband in the kitchen shaking frantically with what looked like a wire running from his waist toward the electric kettle. Intending to jolt him away from the deadly current, she whacked him with a handy plank of wood by the back door, breaking his arm in two places. Until that moment, he had been happily listening to his Walkman.

Two West German motorists suffered a head-on collision in heavy fog near the small town of Guetersloh. Each was driving slowly near the center of the road, and at the moment of impact both their heads were out of the windows. Both men were hospitalized with severe head injuries. Their cars weren't scratched.

After assassinating President Lincoln at Ford's Theater, John Wilkes Booth jumped to the stage. As he jumped, he tripped over an American flag and broke his leg.

A Cuban man was struck by lightning five times in twenty-two years.

Travis Bogumill, a construction worker in Eau Claire, Wisconsin, was shot with a nail gun that drove a 3.5-inch nail all the way into his skull. He was not killed, not even knocked unconscious. The only result from the incident was a decrease in his mathematics skills.

ANIMAL HOUSE

MONKEY BUSINESS

Monkeys fling feces at each other when agitated.

Male rhesus monkeys often hang from tree branches by their prehensile penises.

Chimpanzees live in groups that each have their own culture.

Chimpanzees will hunt ducks if given the opportunity.

To maintain a chimpanzee in captivity for sixty years would cost an estimated $400,000.

Baboons and chimps dig for clean water when the surface water is polluted. Chimps even use sticks as digging tools.

Baboons cannot throw overhand.

Moscow Zoo keepers put televisions in the cages

of their gorillas in an effort to make them "think more."

In 2006, forty-eight orangutans smuggled into a Thai amusement park and forced to participate in mock kick-boxing competitions were returned to their native Indonesia.

QUIRKY TURKEYS

Turkeys were first brought to Britain in 1526 by William Strickland, who sold six, acquired from American Indians, for sixpence each in Bristol.

Only male turkeys gobble. Females make a clicking sound.

Domestic turkeys cannot fly because of their size and breeding, but in the wild, they can fly at up to 50 miles per hour over short distances and run at 20 miles per hour.

The only time a turkey whistles is when it is panicking.

ALMOST HUMAN

A Brazilian politician once drew up a law to ban people from giving their pets "human" names.

A church in Connecticut is giving Holy Communion to pets and offering them special worship services.

A Swiss woman is offering lessons on how to talk with animals for $500 a session.

Firefighters in Florida are carrying oxygen masks for cats, dogs, and even hamsters to help save pets suffering from smoke inhalation.

A Michigan woman who runs a boutique for pets is stocking a special range of Halloween costumes for dogs.

Cash-strapped bosses at Moscow Zoo are renting out animals for the day in an effort to boost funds.

A Belgian company is producing ice cream specifically for dogs.

The London Zoo employs an "entertainment director" for the animals.

A Chilean doctor is using alternative medicines to treat pets and their owners for mental conditions including depression.

A Brazilian vet is offering plastic surgery and Botox injections for pampered pets.

The world's first restaurant for cats operated for four days in New York in 2004.

A Catholic priest has started holding masses for pets in the German city of Cologne.

A Brazilian seaside town has built two toilets for dogs to try to stop pets from fouling the beach.

New Zealand has abandoned plans for a flatulence tax on animals in the face of fierce opposition from farmers.

A Brazilian company is launching a chewing gum for dogs.

The United Kingdom's first canine classroom assistant has been appointed to a school in Derbyshire.

A gym exclusively for dogs has opened in Santiago, Chile.

A chain of gyms has started offering yoga classes for dogs.

BIRD BRAINS

Ravens can learn to open a box to get a treat, and then teach others to do the same.

Finches practice songs in their sleep.

When mating, a hummingbird's wings beat two hundred times a second.

A flock of swallows has delayed more than one hundred flights after taking over a runway at Beijing International Airport.

The average male American bald eagle weighs about nine pounds.

Robins eat three miles of earthworms in a year.

THERE'S NO PLACE LIKE HOME . . .

A British homing pigeon became a star after completing a 3,321-mile journey across the Atlantic.

Homing pigeons use roads where possible to help find their way home, but are becoming increasingly lost because of cell phone towers, say racing enthusiasts.

The top speed of a pigeon in flight is 60 miles per hour.

If birds could sweat, they wouldn't be able to fly.

A gizzard or gosherd is a person who owns geese.

In 2004 Scottish scientists were the first in the world to breed a golden eagle chick from frozen sperm.

Trained hawks were employed to keep pigeons from making a mess on visitors in Manhattan's Bryant Park but were grounded in August 2003 because one of the birds attacked a Chihuahua. The dog survived.

🌰 FLIGHTLESS FOLLIES

Emus cannot walk backward.

Ostriches can run faster than horses and the males can roar like lions.

Penguins can jump as high as six feet out of the water.

AQUATIC ADVENTURES

The Antarctic cod icefish has a protein in its blood that acts like antifreeze and stops the fish from freezing in icy water.

Fish are much brainier than previously thought—and can learn more quickly than dogs.

Tish, the world's oldest captive goldfish, died in his bowl in 1999, forty-three years after being won at a Yorkshire fair. Another fish, Goldie, was supposedly forty-five when he died in 2005, but with no documented proof, Tish retains the title.

The Amazon River is home to the world's only nut- and seed-eating fish.

Most marine fish can survive in a tank filled with human blood.

🌰 SHARK ATTACK!

Blue sharks can give birth to as many as one hundred pups per litter.

The megalodon shark became extinct about 1.6 million years ago. Marine biologists have estimated the megalodon shark was double the size and weight of today's great white shark.

The world's only robotic swimming shark, called Roboshark, lives in a specially designed aquarium at National Marine Aquarium in Plymouth, England.

The shortfin mako shark is the fastest fish in the ocean, clocking speeds of up to 46 miles per hour.

Sharks have a special sensory organ called the "ampullae of Lorenzini" that allows them to detect the electromagnetic field of other organisms.

BLOW IT OUT YOUR HOLE!

The heart of a blue whale only beats nine times a minute.

A blue whale's testicles are the size of a family car.

A Weddell seal can hold its breath for approximately eighty minutes.

SHELF THIS SHELLFISH

Cone shell mollusks are just two inches long but have a deadly poison-filled harpoonlike tooth that spears their prey, injecting it with lethal toxins.

Lobsters come in a variety of colors including the normal blue green, yellow, blue, or even white. They don't become red until they are cooked.

Lobsters can regenerate legs, claws, and antennae. In fact, they will sometimes do so intentionally in order to escape a dangerous situation.

Lobsters will sometimes eat each other in captivity and will also eat their discarded shells after molting.

A sea hare can lay forty thousand eggs in one minute.

JUNK IN THE TRUNK

The average pregnancy of an Indian elephant lasts 650 days.

An elderly elephant in Thailand who had lost her teeth was fitted with custom-made dentures.

Mary the Elephant, also known as Mighty Mary, was the victim of the only known elephant hanging in history after she killed her keeper in 1916.

Ruby, an elephant who lived at the Phoenix Zoo, enjoyed painting. One of her paintings sold for $100,000.

Baby elephants can drink more than 20 gallons of milk a day.

Thailand's prime minister has banned vagrant elephants from the streets of Bangkok in an effort to ease traffic chaos.

THE BEAR NECESSITIES

It is believed among Inupiaq Eskimos that all polar bears are left-handed. While this does not appear to be entirely true, it does seem that most polar bears tend to favor their left paws.

Some polar bears turn green a result of algae growing in their fur.

Polar bear fur is not white, it's clear. Polar bear skin is actually black. Their hair is hollow and acts like fiber optics, directing sunlight to warm their skin.

A polar bear can consume up to one hundred pounds of blubber in a single sitting.

A zoo in India served brandy to black bears to keep them warm in winter.

A hibernating bear can go as long as six months without a toilet break.

The gall bladder of the black bear can fetch several thousand dollars on the black market. It is sought for its supposed healing properties.

Very few adult black bears die from natural causes, most finding their end as the result of some human interference.

WHAT'S BLACK AND WHITE OR RED ALL OVER?

Conservation workers have introduced an exercise regime for giant pandas in Chinese zoos because they're too fat to mate.

China has built a cookie factory to cater exclusively to the nutritional needs of its captive giant pandas.

PARTY ANIMALS

Hard-rock music makes termites chew through wood at twice their usual speed.

An experiment in Canada determined that chickens lay more eggs when pop music is played.

Most cows give more milk when they listen to music.

WHAT UP, DOG?

A Chinese man trained his pet dog to walk on its hind legs for up to five miles.

The Basenji, an African dog, is the only dog that does not bark.

One in three dog owners say they have talked to their pets on the phone.

The average American dog will cost its owner $20,000 in its lifetime.

The owner of a German basset hound with the longest dog ears in the world has had them insured for $25,000.

Two dogs were hanged for witchcraft during the Salem witch trials.

Even bloodhounds cannot smell the difference between identical twins.

As of June 2007 a Chihuahua standing 4.9 inches tall and weighing 1.4 pounds has been officially confirmed as the world's smallest living dog. According to the *Guinness Book of World Records*, the smallest dog ever recorded was a 2.8-inch-tall Yorkshire terrier.

A German businessman who trained his dog to perform the Hitler salute was given thirteen months probation.

If an entire family is overweight, it is likely that the dog will be, too.

A Japanese researcher claims dogs can sense earthquakes before they happen.

A three-year-old boxer was dubbed the most allergic dog in Britain after being found to suffer severe allergies to grass, flowers, cotton, lamb, soy, white fish, and most materials used in bedding.

Giving mail carriers training in dog psychology has reduced attacks on them by 80 percent, according to the German post office.

Chocolate affects a dog's heart and nervous system; a few ounces are enough to kill a small dog.

Italy has put border collies, corgis, and St. Bernards on a dangerous-dogs list that bans children and criminals from owning them.

A Japanese department store once offered a special $300 New Year meal for dogs.

Canada's entry in one of the world's most prestigious international art exhibitions in 2003 featured a video filmed by a Jack Russell puppy named Stanley.

Poodles, dachshunds, and Chihuahuas have strutted

down the catwalk at a fashion show organized by a Tokyo department store.

Some dogs can predict when a child will have an epileptic seizure and even protect the child from injury. They're not trained to do this, but simply learn to respond after observing at least one attack.

CREEPY CRAWLIES

Cockroaches can find their way in a dark room by dragging one antenna against the wall.

Crickets hear through their knees.

The giant African cricket enjoys eating human hair.

An ant can detect movement through five centimeters of earth.

Hook-tip moth caterpillars defend their territories by drumming out warnings.

Mosquitoes have teeth.

The world's smallest winged insect is the Tanzanian parasitic wasp. It's smaller than the eye of a housefly.

Until the 1960s, the crosshairs on gun sights were made from spiderweb filaments.

Crickets' chirps vary due to the temperature. For a rough estimate, count the number of chirps in fifteen seconds and then add thirty-seven, and you'll have the temperature in degrees Fahrenheit.

SLIPPERY SERPENTS

Snakes have two sex organs.

A Brazilian man who bought a six-foot boa constrictor online faced charges after it was shipped to him in a paper box.

When snakes are born with two heads, they fight each other for food. The San Diego zoo had a two-headed corn snake named Thelma and Louise, which had fifteen normal offspring.

A snake measuring almost twenty feet long and weighing more than two hundred pounds was once found inside a factory in Brazil.

ANIMAL FARM

In 2006 a British hen laid what might be the world's largest chicken egg, weighing approximately seven ounces.

A chicken's top speed is 9 miles per hour.

Sheep can detect other sheep faces in the way that humans

do. Researchers claim a sheep can remember up to fifty sheep faces.

Croat farmers once staged a beauty contest for goats in an attempt to publicize the fact that traditional goat farming is dying out.

Goat's eyes have rectangular pupils.

Sheep can survive up to two weeks buried in snow-drifts.

Sheep snore.

Black sheep have a better sense of smell than white sheep.

As of 2006 a Yorkshire pig living in New York was the world's largest pig at eight feet long and 1,600 pounds, almost three times the weight of normal adult male pigs.

A German potbellied pig called Berta passed an audition to star in an opera.

Farm animals have been banned from public housing in Kiev after a survey found residents were keeping more than three thousand pigs, five hundred cows, and one thousand goats.

The United States has never lost a war in which mules were used.

🐚 DON'T HAVE A COW!

Cows drink anywhere from 25 to 50 gallons of water each day.

A dairy cow gives nearly 200,000 glasses of milk in her lifetime.

A cow's stomach has four distinct compartments.

To get a gallon of milk, it takes about 345 squirts from a cow's udder.

Conveners of an Australian agricultural show were so concerned at the rise of cosmetic surgery among cattle breeders that they issued new rules forbidding it.

RODENT REVELATIONS

The world's oldest mouse lived until the age of four and was named Yoda.

Giant rats have been trained to sniff out land mines in Tanzania.

Male and female rats may have sex twenty times a day.

Rats destroy an estimated third of the world's food supply each year.

A study has concluded that if a woodchuck could chuck wood it could chuck about 700 pounds.

SQUIRRELED AWAY

Red squirrels are being given rope bridges to help them cross busy roads in some British towns.

Research suggests that squirrels have the equivalent of "red green" color blindness.

A squirrel's brain is approximately the size of a walnut.

Camel hairbrushes are often made from squirrel hair.

CULINARY CUSTOMS

SPIRITED AWAY

There is a bar in London that sells vaporized vodka, which is inhaled instead of sipped.

To cure hangovers, people in the Middle Ages would down a plate of bitter almonds and dried eel after drinking. In Outer Mongolia, they slurped down pickled sheep eyeballs in tomato juice.

TRIVIA ON TAP

Legend has it that when Burmese women are making beer, they need to avoid having sex or the beer will be bitter.

In the thirteenth century, Europeans baptized children with beer.

Weekend beer drinkers in Dublin consume 9,800 pints an hour between 5:30 p.m. Friday and 3 a.m. on Monday.

Before Prohibition, the most common method of drinking beer at home was drinking it out of a bucket filled at a local pub or brewery.

A BREAKFAST BREAK

Americans buy 2.7 billion packages of breakfast cereal each year. If laid end to end, the empty cereal boxes from one year's consumption would stretch to the moon and back.

Americans consume about ten pounds, or 160 bowls, of cereal per person each year. But the United States ranks only fourth in per capita cereal consumption. Ireland ranks first, England is second, and Australia third.

The cereal industry uses 816 million pounds of sugar per year, enough to coat each and every American with more than three pounds of sugar. The cereal with the highest amount of sugar per serving is Smacks, which is 53 percent sugar.

In the 1820s, a temperance movement tried to ban coffee and nearly succeeded.

Nearly 49 percent of Americans start each morning with a bowl of cereal, 30 percent eat toast, 28 percent eat eggs, 28 percent have coffee, 17 percent have hot cereal, and fewer than 10 percent have pancakes, sausage, bagels, or French toast.

🎺 EGG ON YOUR FACE

The world's largest omelet was made in Canada in 2002 and weighed 6,510 pounds.

Boiled eggs are the most popular way to eat eggs in Britain, followed by scrambled then fried.

THE SWEET LIFE

The largest pumpkin pie ever made weighed 2,020 pounds and was baked in Ohio in 2005.

Chocolate was used as medicine during the eighteenth century. It was believed that chocolate could cure a stomachache. Chocolate contains phenethylamine, the same chemical that your brain produces when you fall in love.

It is a popular theory that Hershey's Kisses are named for the way the machine that makes them looks like it's kissing the conveyor belt. Even the company doesn't know for sure whether it's true.

The world's oldest piece of chewing gum is nine thousand years old.

Great Britain consumes the most ice cream of any European country.

A sixty-eight-year-old Illinois man received a fifteen-month jail sentence for labeling a 530-calorie doughnut as low-fat.

MICKEY'S MINUTIAE

The first McDonald's opened in 1940 in San Bernardino, California. By 1970 there was a McDonald's in every state.

McDonald's is the single largest purchaser of beef, pork, potatoes, and apples in the United States.

According to the Golden Arches Theory of Conflict Prevention, no two countries have fought a war against one another since each got its McDonald's. The accuracy of this statement depends on a flexible interpretation of the term "war."

There are 1,008 McDonald's franchises in France.

McDonald's calls frequent buyers of their food heavy users.

Forty percent of McDonald's profits come from the sale of Happy Meals.

FOOD FAVORITES

Fast-food provider Hardee's Monster Thickburger has 1,420 calories and 107 grams of fat.

Iceland consumes more Coca-Cola per capita than any other nation.

Farmers in Japan have developed square watermelons because they stack better.

Charles Lindbergh took only four sandwiches with him on his famous transatlantic flight.

At one time, pumpkins were recommended for the removal of freckles and curing snakebites.

The biggest pumpkin in the world weighed 1,502 pounds.

Henry VIII was the first British king to eat turkey at Christmas but Edward VII made it fashionable.

The longest sausage made in Australia was 6.9 miles long.

Fifty-eight percent of American schoolkids say pizza is their favorite cafeteria food.

All fruits have three layers: exocarp (skin), mesocarp (pulp), and endocarp (pit).

The peach was the first fruit eaten on the moon.

Thirty-two out of thirty-three samples of well-known brands of milk purchased in Los Angeles and

Orange counties in California had trace amounts of perchlorate, which is the explosive component in rocket fuel.

If you place a T-bone steak in a bowl of Coke, it will be gone in two days. The citric acid in Coke also removes stains from vitreous china. Pour a can into the toilet bowl and let it sit for one hour, then flush clean.

ACQUIRED TASTES

Acorns were used as a coffee substitute during the Civil War.

The ancient Greeks slaughtered sheep and ate the entrails while they were still warm.

The Romans ate fried canaries.

MARRIAGE MUSINGS

"The world has suffered more from the ravages of ill-advised marriages than from virginity."

Ambrose Bierce

"Many a man owes his success to his first wife and his second wife to his success."

Jim Backus

"Marriage is the one subject on which all women agree and all men disagree."

Oscar Wilde

"If you want to sacrifice the admiration of many men for the criticism of one, go ahead, get married."

Katharine Hepburn

"Long engagements give people the opportunity of finding out each other's character before marriage, which is never advisable."

Oscar Wilde

"Bigamy is having one wife too many. Monogamy is the same."

    Oscar Wilde

"Women might be able to fake orgasms, but men can fake whole relationships."

    Sharon Stone

"Laugh and the world laughs with you. Snore and you sleep alone."

    Anthony Burgess

"I married the first man I ever kissed. When I tell this to my children, they just about throw up."

    Barbara Bush

"Men marry because they are tired, women because they are curious; both are disappointed."

    Oscar Wilde

"No man should marry until he has studied anatomy and dissected at least one woman."

    Honore de Balzac

"An archaeologist is the best husband a woman can have; the older she gets the more interested he is in her."

    Agatha Christie

"The most happy marriage I can imagine to myself would be the union of a deaf man to a blind woman."

    S. T. Coleridge

"The male is a domestic animal, which, if treated with firmness, can be trained to do most things."

Jilly Cooper

"Ah Mozart! He was happily married—but his wife wasn't."

Victor Borge

"If you are afraid of loneliness, don't marry."

Anton Chekhov

"The trouble with some women is that they get all excited about nothing—and then marry him."

Cher

"One survey found that 10 percent of Americans thought Joan of Arc was Noah's wife . . ."

Robert Boynton

"For a male and female to live continuously together is . . . biologically speaking, an extremely unnatural condition."

Robert Briffault

"Husbands are awkward things to deal with; even keeping them in hot water will not make them tender."

Mary Buckley

"Marriage is popular because it combines the maximum of temptation with the maximum of opportunity."

George Bernard Shaw

"The majority of husbands remind me of an orangutan trying to play the violin."

Jonathan Carroll

"If variety is the spice of life, marriage is the big can of leftover Spam."

Johnny Carson

"Better to have loved a short man than never to have loved a tall."

David Chambless

"Marriage is an adventure, like going to war."

G. K. Chesterton

"Marriage is like a bank account. You put it in, you take it out, you lose interest."

Irwin Corey

"I've sometimes thought of marrying, and then I've thought again."

Noel Coward

"I feel like Zsa Zsa Gabor's sixth husband. I know what I'm supposed to do, but I don't know how to make it interesting."

Milton Berle

"I'd marry again if I found a man who had fifteen million

and would sign over half of it to me before the marriage
and guarantee he'd be dead within a year."

Bette Davis

"Never go to bed angry. Stay up and fight."

Phyllis Diller

"It destroys one's nerves to be amiable every day to the
same human being."

Benjamin Disraeli

"Politics doesn't make strange bedfellows, marriage
does."

Groucho Marx

"Honolulu, it's got everything. Sand for the children, sun
for the wife, sharks for the wife's mother."

Ken Dodd

"Any intelligent woman who reads the marriage contract,
and then goes into it, deserves all the consequences."

Isadora Duncan

"A man's wife has more power over him than the state
has."

Ralph Waldo Emerson

"Choose a wife by your ear rather than your eye."

Thomas Fuller

"Marriage is a great institution, but who wants to live in an institution?"

Groucho Marx

"Keep your eyes wide open before marriage, and half-shut afterwards."

Benjamin Franklin

"I was married by a judge. I should have asked for a jury."

Groucho Marx

"Love is an ideal thing, marriage a real thing; a confusion of the real with the ideal never goes unpunished."

Johann Wolfgang von Goethe

"We in the industry know that behind every successful screenwriter stands a woman. And behind her stands his wife."

Groucho Marx

"Love is blind and marriage is the institution for the blind."

James Graham

"Wives are people who feel they don't dance enough."

Groucho Marx

"If I were a girl, I'd despair. The supply of good women far exceeds that of the men who deserve them."

Robert Graves

"A man must marry only a very pretty woman in case he should ever want some other man to take her off his hands."

Sacha Guitry

"Women and cats will do as they please. Men and dogs had better get used to it."

Robert Heinlein

"Sometimes I wonder if men and women really suit each other. Perhaps they should live next door and just visit now and then."

Katharine Hepburn

"Bigamy is one way of avoiding the painful publicity of divorce and the expense of alimony."

Oliver Herford

"Wedding is destiny, and hanging likewise."

John Heywood

"A man who marries a woman to educate her falls a victim to the same fallacy as the woman who marries a man to reform him."

Elbert Hubbard

"Marrying a man is like buying something you've been admiring for a long time in a shop window. You may love it when you get it home, but it doesn't always go with everything in the house."

Jean Kerr

"I don't worry about terrorism. I was married for two years."

Sam Kinison

"A coward is a hero with a wife, kids, and a mortgage."

Marvin Kitman

"Marriage is a lottery, but you can't tear up your ticket if you lose."

F. M. Knowles

"Many a man in love with a dimple makes the mistake of marrying the whole girl."

Stephen Leacock

"Harpo, she's a lovely person. She deserves a good husband. Marry her before she finds one."

Oscar Levant, to Harpo Marx

"It's true that I did get the girl, but then my grandfather always said, 'Even a blind chicken finds a few grains of corn now and then.'"

Lyle Lovett, after marrying Julia Roberts

"Marriages are made in heaven and consummated on Earth."

John Lyly

"The best way to get husbands to do something is to suggest that perhaps they are too old to do it."

Shirley MacLaine

"In a novel, the hero can lay ten girls and marry a virgin for the finish. In a movie, that is not allowed. The villain can lay anybody he wants, have as much fun as he wants, cheating, stealing, getting rich, and whipping servants. But you have to shoot him in the end."

Herman Mankiewicz

"I belong to Bridegrooms Anonymous. Whenever I feel like getting married, they send over a lady in a housecoat and hair curlers to burn my toast for me."

Dick Martin

"Eighty percent of married men cheat in America. The rest cheat in Europe."

Jackie Mason

"Perfection is what American women expect to find in their husbands . . . but English women only hope to find in their butlers."

W. Somerset Maugham

"There's a way of transferring funds that is even faster than electronic banking. It's called marriage."

James Holt McGavran

"Women want mediocre men, and men are working hard to become as mediocre as possible."

Margaret Mead

"When a man steals your wife, there is no better revenge than to let him keep her."
    Sacha Guitry

"Bachelors know more about women than married men; if they didn't, they'd be married, too."
    H. L. Mencken

"I date this girl for two years—and then the nagging starts: 'I wanna know your name.'"
    Mike Binder

"I recently read that love is entirely a matter of chemistry. That must be why my wife treats me like toxic waste."
    David Bissonette

"Marriage is like a cage; one sees the birds outside desperate to get in, and those inside desperate to get out."
    Michel de Montaigne

"Never be unfaithful to a lover, except with your wife."
    P. J. O'Rourke

"No woman marries for money; they are all clever enough, before marrying a millionaire, to fall in love with him first."
    Cesare Pavese

"It doesn't much signify whom one marries, for one is sure to find out next morning it was someone else."
    Will Rogers

"Honeymoon: a short period of doting between dating and debting."
    Ray Bandy

"I think men who have a pierced ear are better prepared for marriage. They've experienced pain and bought jewelry."
    Rita Rudner

"To marry is to halve your rights and double your duties."
    Arthur Schopenhauer

"It is most unwise for people in love to marry."
    George Bernard Shaw

"Some of us are becoming the men we wanted to marry."
    Gloria Steinem

"By all means marry. If you get a good wife, you will become happy, and if you get a bad one, you will become a philosopher."
    Socrates

"Marriage: a ceremony in which rings are put on the finger of the lady and through the nose of the gentleman."
    Herbert Spencer

"I think every woman is entitled to a middle husband she can forget."
    Adela Rogers St. John

"Someone once asked me why women don't gamble as

much as men do and I gave the commonsensical reply that we don't have as much money. That was a true but incomplete answer. In fact, women's total instinct for gambling is satisfied by marriage."

Gloria Steinem

"Try praising your wife, even if it does frighten her at first."

Billy Sunday

"Love is blind—marriage is the eye-opener."

Pauline Thomason

"Men have a much better time of it than women: for one thing they marry later, for another thing they die earlier."

H. L. Mencken

"Whenever I date a guy, I think, Is this the man I want my children to spend their weekends with?"

Rita Rudner

"God help the man who won't marry until he finds a perfect woman, and God help him still more if he finds her."

Benjamin Tillett

"A successful man is one who makes more money than his wife can spend. A successful woman is one who can find such a man."

Lana Turner

"Marriage isn't a word . . . it's a sentence."

King Vidor

"I guess the only way to stop divorce is to stop marriage."

Will Rogers

"I take my wife everywhere I go. She always finds her way back."

Henny Youngman

"Marriage is the alliance of two people, one of whom never remembers birthdays and the other who never forgets them."

Ogden Nash

"In olden times, sacrifices were made at the altar, a practice which is still very much practiced."

Helen Rowland

"An ideal wife is one who remains faithful to you but tries to be just as charming as if she weren't."

Sacha Guitry

"I should like to see any kind of a man, distinguishable from a gorilla, that some good and even pretty woman could not shape a husband out of."

Oliver Wendell Holmes Sr.

"A husband is what's left of the lover after the nerve has been extracted."

Helen Rowland

"It does not matter what you do in the bedroom as

long as you do not do it in the street and frighten the horses."

Mrs. Patrick Campbell

"A happy home is one in which each spouse grants the possibility that the other may be right, though neither believes it."

Don Fraser

"Before marriage, a man will lay down his life for you; after marriage he won't even lay down his newspaper."

Helen Rowland

"I've been asked to say a couple of words about my husband, Fang. How about 'short' and 'cheap'?"

Phyllis Diller

"When a girl marries, she exchanges the attentions of many men for the inattention of one."

Helen Rowland

"Sexiness wears thin after a while and beauty fades, but to be married to a man who makes you laugh every day, ah, now that's a real treat."

Joanne Woodward

"Before marriage, a man will lie awake all night thinking about something you said; after marriage, he'll fall asleep before you finish saying it."

Helen Rowland

"The big difference between sex for money and sex for free is sex for money costs less."

Brendan Francis

"To our wives and sweethearts . . . and may they never meet."

Hugo Vickers

"Marriage is like putting your hand into a bag of snakes in the hope of pulling out an eel."

Leonardo da Vinci

"The appropriate age for marriage is around eighteen for girls and thirty-seven for men."

Aristotle

"Instead of getting married again, I'm going to find a woman that I don't like and just give her the house."

Rod Stewart

"When you see what some girls marry, you realize how they must hate to work for a living."

Helen Rowland

"Marriage is one of the few institutions that allows a man to do as his wife pleases."

Milton Berle

THE MOST GROSS

URINE LUCK!

In extreme circumstances runners can drink urine to replace electrolytes.

In pre-colonial Peru, the Incas washed their children's hair with urine as a remedy for head lice.

Navy SEALs sometimes urinate in their pants during cold-water training exercises in order to stay warm.

Urinating on someone or being urinated on for enjoyment is known in fetish parlance as "water sports."

In Minnesota, the Downtown Minneapolis Neighborhood Association has initiated a campaign to prevent or eliminate public urination, which is considered a "quality of life" criminal offense in most cities.

The people of Siberia consumed a hallucinogenic mushroom called *amanita muscaria*, also know as fly agaric. The mushroom's hallucinogenic compound "muscanol" is excreted in the urine intact. When the mushroom was in short supply, the poor would sometimes drink the urine of the wealthy who could afford the mushrooms to experience the hallucinogenic effects themselves.

Wolves, bears, apes, and other mammals use urine to claim territory and communicate eligibility for mating, body size, and other individual characteristics.

In his final book, Sigmund Freud claimed that civilization became possible only when ancient peoples resisted the impulse to extinguish their campfires by pissing them out.

Drinking urine is part of many nontraditional remedies used today, especially in Ayurvedic medicine.

GOING COMMANDO

There are more than 3,500 bras hanging behind the bar at Hogs and Heifers, a bar in Manhattan. So many, in fact, that they caused a beam to collapse in the ceiling.

About 3.9 percent of all American women say they never wear underwear.

THE INTERNET IS FOR PORN

For every "normal" webpage, there are five porn pages.

The most searched term on Yahoo.com every year is "porn."

Passengers at an Indian airport were once shocked when a hard-core porn movie was played on television screens for twenty minutes.

GAS PASSED

On average, humans fart once per hour.

Farts are highly flammable.

Adults produce between two hundred milliliters and two liters of wind per day.

Flatulence is increased by stress and foods such as onions, cabbage, and beans.

Vegetarians fart more. However, their flatulence tends to be less odorous.

On average, a fart is composed of about 59 percent nitrogen, 21 percent hydrogen, 9 percent carbon dioxide, 7 percent methane, and 4 percent oxygen. Less than 1 percent of a fart is made up of odorous gases.

The temperature of a fart at the time of creation is 98.6 degrees F.

Farts have been clocked at a speed of 10 feet per second.

Bernard Clemmens of London managed to sustain a fart for an officially recorded time of 2 minutes 42 seconds.

The word "fart" comes from the Old English "feortan" (meaning "to break wind").

If a person farted consistently for six years and nine months, enough gas would be produced to create the energy of an atomic bomb.

Scuba divers cannot pass gas at depths of thirty-three feet or below.

BIRTHDAY SUITS

A party boat filled with sixty men and women once capsized in Texas after all the passengers rushed to one side as the boat passed a nude beach.

The word "gymnasium" derives from the original Greek noun *gymnasion*. This word was in turn derived from the adjective *gymnos*, which means "naked" (because ancient Greeks undressed for exercise), and from the related Greek word *gymnazein*, which means "to do physical exercise."

FLUSHED AWAY

Ninety-eight percent of all Americans feel better about themselves when they flush a toilet.

> About a third of all Americans flush the toilet while they're still sitting on it.

More toilets flush at the halftime of the Super Bowl than at any other time of the year.

PAPER PREFERENCES

A Kimberly-Clark marketing survey on bathroom habits finds that, when it comes to toilet paper, women are "wadders" and men are "folders."

About 72.4 percent of people place their toilet paper on the roll facing forward (with the loose end over the roll, toward the user).

The visitors at Yellowstone Park create 270 million gallons of waste per year and use up to eighteen rolls of toilet paper per toilet per day.

EVERYBODY POOPS

On average, a person produces half a pound of feces per day.

> Dinosaur droppings are called coprolites.

DOING THE NASTY

Each day, there are more than 120 million acts of sexual intercourse taking place all over the world.

Sex is the safest tranquilizer in the world. It is ten times more effective than valium.

Sex helps sweat out booze.

The biochemical response to sex is the same as eating large quantities of chocolate.

A man's beard grows fastest when he anticipates sex.

The French have topped a survey as being the people who have sex the most.

Women who read romance novels have sex twice as often as those who don't.

SAFE SEX SPECIFICS

The world's oldest preserved condoms were discovered in an ancient toilet in England's Dudley Castle in 1985. They were made from fish and animal intestines and dated back to 1640.

In India, it is cheaper to have sex with a prostitute than to buy a condom.

Casanova wore condoms made of linen.

The average shelf life of a latex condom is about four years if properly stored in a cool, dry place.

PENILE IS MORE THAN JUST A RIVER IN EGYPT

A man became a tourist attraction in the Dominican Republic after admitting himself to the hospital with an erection that had lasted six days.

A German who borrowed $10,000 from his mother for a penis extension demanded a refund after it ended up shorter and deformed.

It is estimated that the Pentagon spent $50 million on Viagra for American troops and veterans in 1999.

"Ithyphallophobia" is a morbid fear of seeing, thinking about, or having an erect penis.

SEX AND MARRIAGE

The first couple to be shown in bed together on prime-time television was Fred and Wilma Flintstone.

Eighty-five percent of men who die of heart attacks during intercourse are found to have been cheating on their wives.

In Kentucky, 50 percent of the people who get married for the first time are teenagers.

A couple from Germany went to a fertility clinic to find out why—after eight years of marriage—they were still childless. The cause of their trouble conceiving was that they never had sex.

ANIMAL URGES

Termites are the largest producers of farts.

Formicophilia is the fetish for having small insects crawl on your genitals.

Some lions mate more than fifty times a day.

Spotted skunks do handstands before they spray.

CRIMINAL COPULATION

If a police officer in Coeur d'Alene, Idaho, suspects a couple are having sex inside a vehicle he must honk his horn three times and wait two minutes before approaching the scene.

A law in Oblong, Illinois, makes it a crime to make love while fishing or hunting on your wedding day.

In Ames, Iowa, a husband may not take more than three gulps of beer while lying in bed with his wife.

A law in Alexandria, Minnesota, makes it illegal for a

husband to make love to his wife if his breath smells like garlic, onions, or sardines.

A Helena, Montana, law states that a woman cannot dance on a saloon table unless her clothing weighs more than three pounds two ounces.

Hotel owners in Hastings, Nebraska, are required by law to provide a clean, white cotton nightshirt to each guest. According to the law, no couple may have sex unless they are wearing the nightshirts.

Any couple making out inside a vehicle, and accidentally sounding the horn during their lustful act, may be taken to jail, according to a law in Liberty Corner, New Jersey.

During lunch breaks in Carlsbad, New Mexico, a couple is breaking the law if they engage in a sexual act while parked in their vehicle, unless their car has curtains.

In Harrisburg, Pennsylvania, it is illegal to have sex with a truck driver inside a toll booth.

In Kingsville, Texas, there is a law against two pigs having sex on the city's airport property.

A Tremonton, Utah, law states that no woman is allowed to have sex with a man while riding in an ambulance. In addition to normal charges, the woman's name will be published in the local newspaper. The man does not receive any punishment.

In the state of Washington, there is a law against having sex with a virgin under any circumstances (including the wedding night).

The only acceptable sexual position in Washington, DC, is the missionary-style position. Any other sexual position is considered illegal.

JUST PLAIN GROSS

The study of nose picking is called rhinotillexomania.

One of the most difficult items for sewage workers to handle, as it is insoluble yet fine enough to pass through most filtration systems, is pubic hair. Every month Thames Water in England removes more than a ton of pubic hair at its water-treatment plants, whereupon it is taken away to a landfill site and buried.

Seven percent of Americans claim they never bathe at all.

HISTORICAL RECORDS

DOLLARS AND SENSE

As of January 2004, the United States economy borrows $1.4 billion each day from foreign investors.

The New York City Police Department has a $3.3 billion annual budget, larger than all but nineteen of the world's armies.

The House of Representatives earmarked $180 million to create an indoor rain forest in Iowa.

In 2005, Congress earmarked $223 million for a bridge in Alaska that would connect the mainland to Gravina Island, population fifty. The so-called Bridge to Nowhere would be taller than the Brooklyn Bridge and longer than the Golden Gate.

LAWS WITHOUT CAUSE

Texas is the only state that permits residents to cast absentee ballots from space.

Legislators in Santa Fe, New Mexico, are considering a law that would require pets to wear seat belts when traveling in a car.

THE RESULTS ARE IN . . .

The day after President George W. Bush was re-elected in 2004, Canada's main immigration website had 115,000 visitors. Before Bush's re-election, this site averaged about 20,000 visitors each day.

The fertility rate in states that voted for George W. Bush is 12 percent higher than states that favored John Kerry in the 2004 presidential election.

CNN's coverage of John Kerry's acceptance speech at the 2004 Democratic National Convention was marred by the accidental broadcast of expletives from a technician.

In 2004, John Kerry's hometown newspaper, the *Lowell Sun*, endorsed George W. Bush for president. Bush's hometown newspaper, the *Lone Star Iconoclast*, endorsed John Kerry for president.

Television networks hung banners at the 2004 Democratic

National Convention, including Al-Jazeera, until it was noticed and taken down.

PRESIDENTS WITHOUT PRECEDENT

Jimmy Carter once reported a UFO in Georgia.

During Bill Clinton's entire eight-year presidency, he only sent two emails. One was to John Glenn when he was aboard the space shuttle, and the other was a test of the email system.

The Oval Office is thirty-five feet long.

George Washington is the only president to have been unanimously elected.

Zachary Taylor never voted until the age of sixty-two. He had moved around too often as a soldier to establish a place of permanent residence.

John Quincy Adams was known to swim nude in the Potomac River.

PRESIDENTIAL FIRSTS

Martin Van Buren was the first president to be born in the United States (after the ratification of the Constitution).

Andrew Jackson was the first president to ride in a train.

James K. Polk was the first president to host a Thanksgiving dinner.

Franklin Pierce was the first president to ask for a Christmas tree in the White House.

Benjamin Harrison was the first president to have electricity in the White House.

Herbert Hoover was the first president born west of the Mississippi.

John F. Kennedy was the first president born in the twentieth century.

Jimmy Carter was the first president born in a hospital.

FIVE-STAR FACTS

The Pentagon now has twice as many bathrooms as when it was built in the 1940s.

There are 68,000 miles of phone line in the Pentagon.

More than 8,100 U.S. troops are still listed as missing in action from the Korean War.

A war veteran who got lost on his way back from the D-Day commemorations in 2004 got a lift back to Paris from French President Jacques Chirac.

FUNKY FOUNDING FATHERS

Benjamin Franklin gave guitar lessons.

George Washington spent about 7 percent of his annual salary on liquor.

Thomas Jefferson's headstone reads "Here was buried Thomas Jefferson, author of the Declaration of Independence, of the statute of Virginia for Religious Freedom, and the father of the University of Virginia." There is no mention of his presidency.

REVOLUTIONARY THINKING

"Facts are stubborn things; and whatever may be our wishes, our inclination, or the dictates of our passions, they cannot alter the state of facts and evidence."   John Adams

"Here, sir, the people govern."   Alexander Hamilton

"A republican government is slow to move, yet when once in motion, its momentum becomes irresistible."

Thomas Jefferson

"All men having power ought to be distrusted to a certain degree."   James Madison

"The cause of America is in a great measure the cause of all mankind."   Thomas Paine

"Guard against the impostures of pretended patriotism."

George Washington

"I am not a Virginian, but an American."   Patrick Henry

"I only regret that I have but one life to lose for my country."
Nathan Hale

"My hand trembles, but my heart does not."
Stephen Hopkins, upon signing the
Declaration of Independence

"There! His Majesty can now read my name without glasses.
And he can double the reward on my head!"
John Hancock, upon signing the
Declaration of Independence

IT'S ALL GREEK TO ME . . . OR RUSSIAN . . . OR FRENCH . . .

Norway's Crown Prince Haakon placed Portugal on the Mediterranean in a welcome speech for the country's president.

Greek officials had to apologize after dropping a 113-year-old man from an electoral register because they refused to believe he was still alive.

About 1,600 Belgians turned out to vote in the country's elections wearing only swimming suits or trunks.

In 2003 the French government banned the use of the word "email" in all its ministries, documents, publications, and websites in favor of the word "courriel," a fusion of the words "courrier electron-ique" (electronic mail).

India has an estimated 550 million voters.

LEAGUE OF NATIONS

Charles de Gaulle was wounded while serving in World War I and captured by German troops. After five un-successful escape attempts, he was transferred to a high-security prison camp.

In his youth, Tony Blair was in a rock band.

Former Ugandan dictator Idi Amin was the heavyweight champion of that country from 1951 to 1960.

Former UN Secretary General Kofi Annan's last name is often mispronounced. The correct pronunci-ation rhymes with "cannon."

The founder of the FBI, Charles Joseph Bonaparte, was a grandnephew of Napoleon.

Japan's World War II leader, Hideki Tojo, was nick-named "Razor."

Nehru jackets are so called after the first Indian Prime Minister, Jawaharlal Nehru, whose wardrobe inspired their design.

The name of Libya's leader is spelled in more than thirty different ways in the press, including Muammar al-Gaddafi, Mu'ammar Qaddafi, Moammar Gadhafi, and Muammer Khadafy.

✇ UNCLE JOE

Stalin studied in a seminary in his youth, until he was expelled.

Stalin was only five feet four inches tall.

Stalin's only daughter, Svetlana Alliluyeva Stalina, is still alive and living in a retirement home in Wisconsin.

In 1940, Stalin issued the order to have his ally-turned-rival Leon Trotsky assassinated in Mexico. He was killed by an ice pick to the head.

BAD REPS

Norwegian politician Trond Helleland was once caught playing games on his handheld computer during a debate in parliament.

A Brazilian politician lost his seat over allegations that he offered voters free Viagra in exchange for their support.

UK Conservative politician John Bercow sold his eighteenth-century home because his long-legged fiancée kept bumping her head on the low ceilings.

PRISON BLUES

Frank Wathernam was the last prisoner to leave Alcatraz Prison, on March 21, 1963.

A Czech prisoner locked up on theft charges was freed and allowed to go back home to his wife after getting a permanent erection.

The prisoners of a small Brazilian jail are paying the bills in exchange for better conditions.

Germany has drawn up blueprints for Europe's first jail specifically to house OAPs—old-aged prisoners.

Classical music and aromatherapy are being used in a Mexican jail to try to calm down some of the most dangerous prisoners.

In a stroke of irony, the maximum-security prison in St. Albans, Vermont, was responsible in 1996 for sending out public-relations brochures enticing tourists to visit Vermont.

Four jails in Brazil are using geese to help prevent prisoners from escaping.

To help reduce budget deficits, several states have begun reducing the amount of food served to prison inmates. In Texas, the number of daily calories served to prisoners was cut by 300, saving the state $6 million per year.

AMERICAN PRISONS: BY THE NUMBERS

About 0.7 percent of Americans are currently in prison.

The United States puts more of its citizens in prison than any other nation.

The United States has 5 percent of the world's population, but 25 percent of the world's prison population.

The prison system is the largest supplier of mental-health services in the United States, with 250,000 Americans with mental illness living there.

STRANGE STATUTES

You can be imprisoned for not voting in Fiji, Chile, and Egypt—at least in theory.

In Texas, an anticrime law requires criminals to give their victims twenty-four hours' notice, either orally or in writing, and to explain the nature of the crime to be committed.

In Chico, California, the city council enacted a ban on nuclear weapons, setting a $500 fine for anyone detonating one within city limits.

In ancient Egypt, killing a cat was a crime punishable by death.

In Hong Kong, a betrayed wife is legally allowed to kill her adulterous husband, but may only do so with her bare hands.

Men in Costa Rica can now be sent to prison for trying to hit on women.

In Alaska, it is legal to shoot bears. However, waking a sleeping bear for the purpose of taking a photograph is prohibited.

It is a criminal offense to drive around in a dirty car in Russia.

In Bangladesh, kids as young as fifteen can be jailed for cheating on their finals.

A woman was chewing what was left of her chocolate bar when she entered a Metro station in Washington, DC. She was arrested and handcuffed, as eating is prohibited in Metro stations.

UNJUST JUDGMENTS?

Police in Finland have issued a $200,000 fine to a man who was caught exceeding a 25-mile-per-hour speed limit.

The average length for a criminal sentence in Colombia is 137 years.

A robber was jailed for twelve years in Illinois—despite singing to the court in an effort to get a reduced sentence.

A German man faced up to ten years in a Turkish prison because his nine-year-old son picked up pebbles from a beach. He was charged with smuggling archaeologically valuable national treasures.

An Argentinean man was cleared of urinating on the steps of a museum because they were already dirty.

A Texas prisoner who threw his feces over a prison officer was sentenced to an additional fifty years in prison for harassment.

A Bolivian man spent two months in jail charged with smuggling cocaine before tests revealed he had in fact been carrying talcum powder.

An Iranian man who struck a suicide pact with his new bride over their guilt for having premarital sex was held by police after he backed out of his side of the bargain.

In ancient Greece, an adulterous male was sometimes punished by the removal of his pubic hair and the insertion of a large radish into his rectum.

POLICE DEPARTMENT

Russian police once stopped women drivers to hand out flowers instead of speeding tickets to mark International Women's Day.

Police officers in India have invited the public to post jokes about them in an attempt to improve the image of the force.

More than four hundred policemen in a Mexican city were once ordered to go on a diet. Overweight policemen in the Philippines were ordered to take an antiobesity drug to help the force slim down.

Al Capone's older brother Vince was a policeman in Nebraska.

Two San Francisco police officers were once caught moonlighting in a hard-core porn movie.

Prostitutes in a Dutch city say their business is being ruined by policemen turning up to watch them have sex with clients.

AIRPORT REPORT

British customs officers have arrested an air passenger carrying more than her own weight in edible snails.

Airport security personnel find about six weapons a day by searching passengers.

CRIMINAL MASTERMINDS

An Argentinean burglar who got stuck in a chimney was ordered to rebuild it himself.

A Belgium news agency reported that a man suspected of robbing a jewelry store in Liège said he couldn't have done it because he was busy breaking into a school at the same time. Police then arrested him for breaking into the school.

A couple caught on camera robbing a store could not be identified until the police reviewed the security tape. The woman had filled out an entry form for a free trip prior to robbing the store.

A Romanian man jailed four years earlier for burgling a wealthy neighbor's apartment was caught by the same policeman robbing the same property hours after he was released from jail.

Wayne Black, a suspected thief, had his name tattooed across his forehead. When confronted by police, Black insisted he wasn't Wayne Black. To prove it, he stood in front of a mirror and insisted he was Kcalb Enyaw.

A prisoner in Decatur, Georgia, fell through the roof

of a courthouse and into a judge's chambers while trying to escape.

A drunken German who bought three hand grenades at a flea market in Bosnia was arrested after throwing one out of the window to see whether it worked.

An Englishman who shot himself in the groin was jailed for five years for illegal possession of a firearm.

Thieves who stole a public toilet in the Belarus city of Gomel accidentally kidnapped a man still locked inside.

A female student once came home to find a drunken burglar in her apartment, wearing her clothes.

A Buddhist monk decided to break his lifelong vow of celibacy with a prostitute, but picked up an undercover police officer instead.

CRIME NOTES

Quebec City, Canada, has about as much street crime as Disney World.

Two-thirds of the world's kidnappings occur in Colombia.

The average number of cars stolen per day in Mexico City is 124.

A magician's rabbit was "liberated" mid-act by a suspected animal-rights activist in Brighton, England.

A man was arrested and charged with the robbery of vending machines. The man posted his bail entirely in quarters.

A gentleman mugger in Austria was jailed despite his elderly victim's pleas for him to be let off because he was so polite.

In September 2004, a Minnesota state trooper issued a speeding ticket to a motorcyclist who was clocked at 205 miles per hour.

A Chinese truck driver was arrested for kidnapping two toll-station operators to save the equivalent of $1.50.

Russians reportedly pay out more than $40 billion a year in bribes, with the average person paying almost a tenth of his wages in bribes.

A sketch of a burglar drawn by an eleven-year-old schoolboy was so good it allowed Austrian police to catch the thief less than an hour later.

Hondas and Toyotas are the most frequently stolen passenger cars because they have parts that can be readily exchanged between model years without a problem.

Police in Canada impounded an ambulance after arresting the driver for trying to pick up a prostitute.

Police in Germany had to rescue a swimming-pool attendant at a bachelorette party after the bride-to-be tried to bully him into having sex.

NEWS OF THE WORLD

A British woman married a man just a month after he stabbed her for having pre-wedding jitters.

A New York woman reportedly fended off her husband's violent sexual advances by setting him on fire.

A judge in the United States was dismissed after using a penis pump while trying cases in court.

There are at least two reported instances of British college students auctioning off their virginity on eBay.

A Romanian man was charged with trying to blow up his kitchen because his wife was a lousy cook.

A German man who faked his death so he could leave his family for a younger woman was fined $20,000.

Police believe a teenager in Romania who crashed a car into a telephone pole was having sex with his girlfriend at the time.

A groom was given away at his wedding by his ex-wife—and his best man was his ex's new boyfriend.

Croatian monks have been ordered to sell off their BMWs and Mercedes.

Residents of an Austrian village called Fucking voted against changing the name in 2004, but did replace their road signs with theft-resistant versions welded to steel and secured in concrete to stem their frequent theft. (The name is pronounced to rhyme with "looking.")

THE BEGUILING
BARD

"I BEAR A CHARMED LIFE . . ."

William Shakespeare was born to a Stratford glover and alderman named John Shakespeare. His mother, Mary, was the daughter of a wealthy gentleman farmer named Robert Arden.

There is no certainty that Shakespeare was born on April 23, 1564, only that he was baptized three days later in Holy Trinity Church in Stratford-upon-Avon.

There were two Shakespeare families living in Stratford when William was born; the other family did not become famous.

Some believe that *Hamlet*, written in 1599, registers Shakespeare's grief following the death of his son, Hamnet, in 1596, at the age of eleven.

Legend has it that, at the tender age of eleven, Shakespeare watched the pageantry associated with Queen Elizabeth I's visit to Kenilworth Castle near Stratford and later re-created this scene many times in his plays.

Shakespeare never attended a college or university.

Shakespeare dabbled in property development. At age fifteen, he bought the second most prestigious property in all of Stratford, The New Place, and later he doubled his investment on some land he bought near Stratford. These investments may be what afforded him enough time to devote to his plays.

Anne Hathaway was twenty-six years old when Shakespeare married her at age eighteen.

Shakespeare and his wife had three children. His last surviving descendant was his granddaughter Elizabeth Hall. There are no direct descendents of Shakespeare alive today.

Shakespeare wrote on average 1.5 plays a year from when he first started in 1589.

Even Shakespeare had his critics. One named Robert Greene described the young playwright as an "upstart young crow" or arrogant upstart, accusing him of borrowing ideas from his seniors in the theater world for his own plays.

Shakespeare died in 1616 at the age of fifty-two, apparently from an infection after eating spoiled herring. Unlike most famous artists of his time, he did not die in poverty. When he died, his will contained several large holdings of land.

Shakespeare's will bequeathed most of his property to Susanna, his first child, and not to his wife, Anne. He left Anne his "second-best bed," otherwise known as his marriage bed, as the "best bed" was for guests.

Shakespeare's tombstone bears this inscription: "Good friend, for Jesus' sake forbear to dig the dust enclosed here. Blest be the man that spares these stones, and curst be he that moves my bones."

"WHAT'S IN A NAME?"

In the Middle East, Shakespeare is referred to as Sheikh al-Subair, meaning Sheikh "Prickly Pear" in Arabic.

There are only two authentic portraits of William Shakespeare.

All Uranus's moons are named after Shakespearean characters.

Shakespeare's will is now available to the public to read online, nearly four hundred years after he put quill to paper.

"I HAVE IMMORTAL LONGINGS IN ME . . ."

When reading vertically downward from Shakespeare's original published copy of *Hamlet*, the furthest left-hand side apparently reads "I am a homosexual" in the last fourteen lines of the book.

Many of Shakespeare's sonnets were written to a young man known as the "Fair Lord." His 126th poem contains a farewell to "my lovely boy," a phrase taken to imply possible homosexuality or bisexuality by some postmodern Shakespeare academics.

"THE GOLDEN AGE IS BEFORE US, NOT BEHIND US . . ."

Queen Elizabeth I outlawed wife-beating after 10 p.m.

Brides carried a bouquet of flowers to hide their body odor—hence, the custom today of carrying a bouquet when getting married.

Bread was divided according to status. Workers got the burned bottom of the loaf, the family got the middle, and guests got the top, or "upper crust."

Those with money had plates made of pewter. Food with high acid content caused some of the lead to leach into the food, often causing lead-poisoning death.

THE BEGUILING BARD 193

"BUT MEN ARE MEN, THE BEST SOMETIMES FORGET . . ."

Shakespeare did not have any involvement in publishing any of his plays. We read his plays today only because his fellow actors John Heminges and Henry Condell posthumously recorded his work as a dedication to their fellow actor. Until the First Folio was published seven years after his death in 1616, very little personal information was ever written about him.

> Shakespeare suffered breach of copyright. In 1609, many of his sonnets were published without his permission.

"ALL THE WORLD'S A STAGE . . ."

Theaters during Elizabethan times did not have toilets, nor did the plays have intermissions.

> Elizabethan theaters would raise a flag outside to indicate what the day's feature would be: a black flag indicated tragedy; a red, history; a white, comedy.

". . . AND ALL THE MEN AND WOMEN MERELY PLAYERS"

Hamlet is the largest Shakespearean speaking part, with nearly 1,500 lines.

The play *Cardenio*, based on a tale in *Don Quixote*, that has been credited to Shakespeare and that was performed in his lifetime, has been completely lost. A 1727 play called *Double Falsehood* is claimed to be based on three manuscripts of this lost play.

None of the characters in Shakespeare's plays smoke.

Suicide occurs an unlucky thirteen times in Shakespeare's plays.

Aside from writing 38 plays and composing 154 sonnets, Shakespeare was also an actor who performed many of his own plays as well as those of other playwrights.

"WORDS, WORDS, MERE WORDS . . ."

Shakespeare coined the phrase "the beast with two backs" meaning intercourse in his play *Othello*.

The worst insult that Shakespeare used was "you bull's pizzle."

Most Shakespeare plays employ verse and prose. But, while no play is composed entirely of prose, five plays are written exclusively in verse.

The average American's vocabulary is around 10,000 words—Shakespeare had a vocabulary of more than 29,000 words.

Shakespeare crudely discusses genitalia size in *The Taming of the Shrew* when the character Curtis tells Grumio, "Away, you three-inch fool."

Shakespeare is believed to have started writing the first of his 154 sonnets in 1593 at age twenty-nine. His first poem was *Venus and Adonis* published in the same year.

English expressions such as "elbow room," "love letter," "marriage bed," "puppy dog," "skim milk," "wild goose chase," and "what the dickens" first appeared in print in Shakespeare's works.

Of the 20,138 new words that Shakespeare uses in his plays, sonnets, and narrative poems, his is the first written use of approximately 1,678 of them.

WAYS TO GO

THE GRIM TRUTH

Every day approximately 259,200 people die.

> Eighty percent of deaths in U.S. casinos are caused by sudden heart attacks.

Thirty people a year in Canada, and three hundred people a year in the United States, are killed by trains.

> In 1998, more fast-food employees were murdered on the job than police officers.

Amusement-park attendance goes up after a fatal accident. It seems many people want to ride upon the same ride that killed someone.

> More people in the United States die during the first week of the month than during the last, an increase that may be a result of the abuse of substances purchased with welfare checks that come at the beginning of each month.

Japanese and Chinese people die on the fourth of the month more often than any other dates. The reason may be that they are "scared to death" by the number four. The words four and death sound alike in both Japanese and Chinese.

People with initials that spell out GOD or ACE are likely to live longer than people whose initials spell out words like APE, PIG, or RAT.

WRITE THEM OFF

Poet Hart Crane committed suicide by drowning. While on a steamship, he bid his fellow passengers farewell and jumped overboard.

Writer Eugene Izzi hanged himself from an eleventh-floor window on Michigan Avenue, Chicago. It was possibly an accident while he was researching a scene for a book.

The Japanese writer Yukio Mishima committed suicide in 1979 by disembowelment and decapitation as a protest of the westernization of Japan. He killed himself in front of an assembly of all of the students that he was teaching at a university at that time.

Poet Sylvia Plath committed suicide by inhaling gas from her oven.

Virginia Woolf committed suicide by drowning in 1941.

Writer Sherwood Anderson swallowed a toothpick at a cocktail party. He died of peritonitis on an ocean liner bound for Brazil.

Ernest Miller Hemingway committed suicide with a shotgun.

Margaret Mitchell, author of *Gone With the Wind*, was crossing an Atlanta street on her way to the theater when she was hit by a speeding cab. She died of her injuries five days later.

Playwright Tennessee Williams choked to death on a nose-spray bottle cap that accidentally dropped into his mouth while he was using the spray.

Jane Austen died of Addison's disease in 1871.

PENALTY SHOT

Velma Barfield was the first woman executed in the United States after the restoration of the death penalty in 1967.

Rainey Bethea was the last publicly executed criminal in the United States, and was hanged in 1936.

Bridget Bishop was the first of the supposed witches hanged in Salem, Massachusetts. She was executed on June 10, 1692.

Charles Brooks Jr. was the first criminal to be executed in the United States by lethal injection.

Romanian President Nicolae Ceauşescu was executed in 1989 by firing squad on live television, along with his wife.

Edward Despard was the last executed criminal to be drawn and quartered in England, in 1803.

World War I spy Mata Hari was executed by firing squad; she refused a blindfold and threw a kiss to the executioners.

German spy Josef Jakobs was the last person to be executed in the Tower of London, in 1941.

Kenneth Allen McDuff is thought to be the only person ever freed from death row and then returned after killing again. He was executed by lethal injection on November 17, 1998, in Huntsville, Texas.

French highwayman Nicolas Jacques Pelletier was the first person beheaded with the guillotine.

Julius and Ethel Rosenberg were executed in the electric chair on June 19, 1953. They were the first husband and wife executed in the United States. They had been charged with espionage and spying.

PLAY DEAD

Diver Sergei Chalibashvili attempted a three-and-a-half reverse somersault in the tuck position during the 1983 World University Games. On the way down, he smashed his head on the board and was knocked unconscious. He died after being in a coma for a week.

Cleveland Indian shortstop Raymond Johnson Chapman died in 1920 after being hit in the head by a pitch, becoming the only player ever killed as a result of a major-league baseball game.

Colombian soccer player Andrés Escobar was murdered by unknown thugs, apparently in anger over the accidental goal he had scored for the United States during a 1994 World Cup game.

Russian figure skater Sergei Grinkov died of a heart attack during skating practice in 1995.

WWF wrestler Owen Hart died in 1999 while performing a stunt in the wrestling ring. He was being lowered into the ring by a cable when he fell seventy feet to his death, snapping his neck.

Jockey Frank Hayes died from a heart attack during a race in 1923. His horse, Sweet Kiss, won the race, making Hayes the only deceased jockey to win a race.

Olympic cyclist Knut Jensen died of a fractured skull

during the 1960 Olympics in Rome. In the 93-degree heat, he collapsed from sunstroke and hit his head. He was one of only two athletes to die as a result of Olympic competition.

Spanish bullfighter Joselito was fatally gored fighting his last bull in 1920.

Olympic runner Francisco Lazaro collapsed toward the end of the 1912 Olympic marathon in Stockholm.

Bill Masterton, hockey player for the Minnesota North Stars, fell over backward and hit his head on the ice after being checked during a game against the Oakland Seals in 1968. His is the only death in professional hockey during the modern era.

Laura Patterson, professional bungee jumper, was killed during rehearsals for the Super Bowl at the New Orleans Superdome in 1997. She died of massive head injuries.

Fencer Vladimir Smirnov died of brain damage at the 1982 World Championships. During a match against Matthias Behr, Behr's foil snapped, pierced Smirnov's mask, penetrated his eyeball, and entered his brain. Smirnov died nine days later.

DO-IT-YOURSELF

Vincent Van Gogh shot himself in 1890 and died two days later.

Talk-show host Ray Combs hanged himself on the night of June 2, 1996, with bedsheets in his hospital room while on a seventy-two-hour suicide watch.

Actress Lillian Millicent Entwistle committed suicide in 1932 by jumping from the H of the "Hollywood" sign.

Kiyoko Matsumoto, a nineteen-year-old student, died in 1933 by jumping into the thousand-foot crater of a volcano on the island of Oshima, Japan. This act started a bizarre fashion in Japan and, in the ensuing months, 944 people did the same thing.

... IN PUBLIC

Thich Quang Duc was the Buddhist monk who famously set himself on fire on the streets of Saigon to protest against government persecution of Buddhists in 1963.

Pennsylvanian politician R. Budd Dwyer called a press conference and, in front of spectators and TV cameras, shot himself in the head in 1987. He had been convicted of bribery and conspiracy in federal court and was about to be sentenced.

Newscaster Chris Chubbuck shot herself in the head during a prime-time news broadcast on Florida TV station WXLT-TV in 1974. She died fourteen hours later.

Jim Jones, the leader of a religious cult known as the People's Temple, killed himself in 1978 after watching more than nine hundred of his followers die from the ingestion of Kool-Aid laced with cyanide.

THE ROLE OF A LIFETIME

Clara Blandick, the actress who played Auntie Em in *The Wizard of Oz*, killed herself with sleeping pills and a plastic bag tied over her head in 1962. She was eighty-one years old and suffering from crippling arthritis.

Saturday Night Live luminary John Belushi died of a drug overdose in 1982.

In 1978, actor Gig Young shot and killed his wife of three weeks, Kim Schmidt, then shot himself.

Actor Jack Cassidy died in a fire, while asleep on the couch in his apartment.

Albert Dekker, actor and California legislator, suffocated by hanging from a shower curtain rod while he was hand-cuffed and wearing women's lingerie.

Teleivision star Bob Crane was murdered in his hotel room in 1976.

Horror-filmmaker Michael Findlay was decapitated by a helicopter blade in 1977.

Rock Hudson died of AIDS. He was the first major public figure to announce he had AIDS.

Actor Eric Fleming drowned when his canoe capsized

during the filming of a movie near the headwaters of the Amazon in the Haullaga River, Peru.

Judy Garland took an overdose of sleeping pills in 1969.

Actress Elizabeth Hartman fell to her death from a fifth-floor window in a bizarre echo of a character in her 1966 movie *The Group*.

Margaux Hemingway committed suicide in 1996 with an overdose of a sedative. She was the fifth person in her family to take her own life.

Actor William Holden was found dead in his apartment. He had been drinking, and apparently fell, struck his head on an end table, and bled to death.

John C. Holmes, porn film star, died due to complications from AIDS in 1988.

Bruce Lee died suddenly in 1973 from a swollen brain. His son Brandon Lee was shot by a gun firing blanks, while filming the movie *The Crow*. His missing scenes were later filled in by computer animation.

Actor Vic Morrow died in a helicopter accident on the set of *Twilight Zone: The Movie*.

Actress Jayne Mansfield died in a car accident in 1967.

Her wig flew off on impact, leading to rumors that she had been decapitated.

PROMINENT PERSONS
PASSING ON

Wealthy socialite John Jacob Astor drowned with the "unsinkable" *Titanic*.

Sir Francis Bacon died of pneumonia. He was experimenting with freezing a chicken by stuffing it with snow.

Thomas à Becket, Archbishop of Canterbury, was murdered in the Canterbury cathedral in 1170 by four knights, supposedly on the orders by Henry II.

Calamity Jane died in 1903 from pneumonia following a bout of heavy drinking.

Al Capone died of syphilis in 1947.

Explorer Christopher Columbus died in 1506 from rheumatic heart disease.

Marie Curie, the chemist who discovered radium, died of leukemia, caused by exposure to radiation.

Mass murderer Jeffrey Dahmer was beaten to death with a broomstick by a fellow inmate at the Columbia Correctional Institute.

Jim Fixx, who made jogging popular, died of a heart attack while jogging.

> Harry Houdini died of a ruptured appendix. He died on Halloween.

Socrates was required to drink hemlock to end his life after being found guilty of corrupting the youth of Athens.

> Grigory Rasputin was assassinated in 1916. He had been poisoned with cyanide, shot three times, and thrown into a river.

Scottish rebel Sir William Wallace was executed in 1305 by being hanged for a short time, then he was taken down still breathing and had his bowels torn out and burned. His head was then struck off, and his body divided into quarters, in the punishment known as "hanged, drawn, and quartered."

🌰 FLIGHT FAILURES

Singer Jim Croce was the victim of a plane crash in 1973. The plane crashed into a tree two hundred yards past the end of the runway while taking off from Natchitoches Municipal Airport in Louisiana.

Jessica Dubroff died at the age of seven in 1996 in a plane crash, while attempting to become the youngest pilot to fly cross-country.

Actor Leslie Howard (Ashley Wilkes in *Gone With the Wind*)

was killed when his civilian plane was shot down by German fighter planes during World War II.

WHOOPS!

Philanthropist Anthony J. Drexel III shot himself accidentally while showing off a new gun in his collection to his friends.

Actress Isadora Duncan was killed through accidental strangulation when her scarf caught on a car wheel.

William Huskisson was the first person killed by a train. His death occurred in 1830 when he was attending the opening of the Liverpool–Manchester Railway in Britain. As he stepped on the track to meet the Duke of Wellington, Stephenson's "Rocket" hit him. He died later that day.

Hal Mark Irish was killed in a leap from a hot-air balloon in what was believed to be the first U.S. death from the thrill sport of bungee jumping. Irish fell more than sixty feet to his death on October 29, 1991, after breaking loose from his bungee cord during a demonstration.

Mary Jo Kopechne drowned when the car she was a passenger in, driven by Senator Edward Kennedy, plunged off a bridge in 1969.

In 1964, Mark Maples was the first person to be killed

on a ride at Disneyland. He stood up while riding the Matterhorn Bobsleds and was thrown to his death.

FUNERAL DIRGE

Singer Donny Hathaway committed suicide in 1979 by jumping from his room on the fifteenth floor of New York's Essex House Hotel.

Michael Hutchence, INXS band member, hanged himself with a belt in his room in the Ritz-Carlton Hotel in Sydney, Australia.

Ludwig van Beethoven died in 1827 of cirrhosis of the liver.

Salvatore "Sonny" Bono died after crashing into a tree while skiing in 1998.

Singer Karen Carpenter passed away from heart failure caused by anorexia nervosa, at age thirty-two.

Conor Clapton, son of musician Eric Clapton, fell out of a fifty-third-floor window at the age of five.

Nat King Cole died of complications following surgery for lung cancer.

Trombonist Tommy Dorsey choked to death in his sleep because of food that had lodged in his windpipe.

Marvin Gaye was murdered on his birthday in 1984 by his father.

Musician John Glasscock died of a heart infection caused by an abscessed tooth.

Leslie Harvey, lead guitarist of the Glasgow band Stone the Crows, died after being electrocuted on stage at Swansea's Top Rank Ballroom on May 3, 1972.

Brian Jones, musician and one-time Rolling Stone, drowned in his swimming pool while drunk and on drugs.

Keith Relf, musician in The Yardbirds, was electrocuted while playing guitar.

Singer Selena was shot by the president of her fan club in 1995.

WHAT GOES AROUND COMES AROUND . . .

Joseph Goebbels, the Nazi politician, killed himself along with his wife and five children by poisoning while at Hitler's Berlin bunker in the final days of World War II. Another Nazi politician, Hermann Goering, poisoned himself hours before he was to be executed in 1946.

Rudolf Hess, the last surviving member of Adolf Hitler's inner circle, strangled himself in 1987 with an electrical cord at age ninety-three while he was the only prisoner in Spandau Prison, Berlin.

KINGS AND QUEENS
KICK THE BUCKET

Roman Emperor Claudius Drusus Germanicus Nero stabbed himself with a sword in AD 68.

Attila the Hun bled to death from a nosebleed on his wedding night.

Alexander I of Greece died from blood poisoning after being bitten by his gardener's pet monkey.

Alexander II, czar of Russia 1855–81, was assassinated by a bomb that tore off his legs, ripped open his belly, and mutilated his face.

Catherine the Great, empress of Russia, had a stroke while going to the bathroom.

Cleopatra committed suicide by poison, supposedly from an asp, a venomous snake, in 30 BC.

Pope Johann XII was beaten to death in AD 963, at age eighteen, by the husband of a woman with whom he was having an affair.

EXECUTIVE EXPIRATIONS

Thomas Jefferson died of dysentery in 1826. He died on the fiftieth anniversary of the signing of the Declaration of Independence, and the same day as John Adams.

Alexander Hamilton, former U.S. treasury secretary, was shot in 1804 by U.S. Vice President Aaron Burr in a pistol duel near Weehawken, New Jersey.

William McKinley, twenty-fifth president, died of gangrene. He was shot by an assassin and his wounds were not properly dressed.